T0229572

MODELING
SOFTWARE
BEHAVIOR

A Craftsman's Approach

MODELING SOFTWARE BEHAVIOR

A Craftsman's Approach

Paul C. Jorgensen

CRC Press
Taylor & Francis Group
Boca Raton London New York

CRC Press is an imprint of the
Taylor & Francis Group, an **informa** business

AN AUERBACH BOOK

Auerbach Publications
Taylor & Francis Group
6000 Broken Sound Parkway NW, Suite 300
Boca Raton, FL 33487-2742

Printed in the United States of America on acid-free paper
10 9 8 7 6 5 4 3 2 1

International Standard Book Number: 978-1-4200-8075-9 (Hardback)

Library of Congress Cataloging-in-Publication Data

Jorgensen, Paul.
    Modeling software behavior : a craftsman's approach / Paul C. Jorgensen.
       p. cm.
    Includes bibliographical references and index.
    ISBN 978-1-4200-8075-9 (hard back : alk. paper)
    1. System design. 2. Software architecture. 3. Computer software--Development. I. Title.

QA76.9.S88J72 2009
005.1--dc22
                                                                              2009019975

Visit the Taylor & Francis Web site at
http://www.taylorandfrancis.com

and the Auerbach Web site at
http://www.auerbach-publications.com

Dedication

To Carol, Kirsten, Katia, and grandchildren from A (Abbie) to Z (Zoe) with Hope and Max in between

Contents

Preface

Avvinare is one of my favorite Italian words. It refers to a process that many Italian families perform in autumn when they bottle wine. After buying a demijohn of bulk wine, they rinse out the empty bottles that they have saved during the year. There are always small droplets of water clinging to the sides of a bottle, but it is really difficult to dry them. Instead, they fill a bottle about half full of the wine, and shake it up to dissolve the water into the wine. Next, the wine is funneled into the next bottle, shaken, and poured into another bottle. This continues until all the bottles have been rinsed with wine, and they are ready for bottling. *Avvinare* is the verb that refers to this entire process. How would you translate this word into English? I really don't know, but it won't be easy. Languages evolve to meet the expressive needs of their speakers, and this activity isn't very common in the English-speaking world. To wax esoteric, this is where software engineering meets epistemology.

This book is about the expressive power of various models of system behavior. There are two fundamental types of requirements specification models: those that describe structure, and those that describe behavior. These correspond to two fundamental views of a system: what a system IS, and what a system DOES. Entity/relation models, dataflow diagrams, hierarchy charts, class diagrams, and object diagrams all focus on what a system is—the components, their functionality, and interfaces among them. They emphasize structure. The second type, including decision tables, finite state machines, statecharts, and Petri nets, describes system behavior—what a system does. Models of system behavior have varying degrees of expressive capability, the technical equivalent of being able to express *avvinare* in another language.

We've all seen the cartoons about requirements specification. Perhaps the most widely known one features a harried supervisor who instructs his group to "start coding while I find out what they want." This cartoon is so old, the programmers have coding pads in front of them instead of terminals. More recently, the pointy-haired supervisor in *Dilbert* tells Wally that "we don't have time to gather the product requirements ahead of time," and continues with, "I want you to start designing the product anyway, otherwise it will look like we aren't accomplishing anything."

As Wally sits with his feet on the desk, reading a newspaper, he reflects, "Of all my projects, I like the doomed ones best."

The essence of requirements specification is the intelligent use of models, both structural and behavioral. This book is based on a graduate course on requirements specification that I have given in universities and to companies since the mid-1980s. In that time, and before that during my industrial career (telephone switching systems), I have read and used dozens of textbooks on requirements specification. One thread common to most of them is that they emphasize structural models to the near exclusion of behavioral models. If they cover behavioral models at all, the coverage is brief, and focuses on just one model. I hope to fill this niche—I want my students and my readers to become skilled at using behavioral models, to understand their expressive capabilities, their limitations, and to be able to make appropriate choices among them.

I like to think of models as a conceptual toolbox. Barry Boehm, an eminent software engineer, jokes that if your only tool is a hammer, pretty soon all your problems look like nails. Educators tell us that there are as many as eight different ways that people learn (and think). For example, I am a visual learner: If someone gives me textual directions to their house, I consult the slip of paper constantly. If I draw a map to their house, I can throw the map away and still find them. The toolbox metaphor extends to the essence of craftsmanship. A good tool in the hands of a poor craftsman can be misused. Conversely, becoming a craftsman entails an apprenticeship during which the use of tools is mastered. One of my grandfathers was a Danish cabinetmaker, my father was a tool and die maker, and one of my uncles is an outstanding woodworker (it's still my hobby). I remember my father helping me cut some wood when I was making one of many boyhood boats. After I had sawed furiously (with the wrong saw) and made a poor cut, he handed me the right saw and simply said, "Use the right tool, and let the tool do the work." I pass this advice to you: Use the right behavioral model, and let the model do the work.

Paul C. Jorgensen, Ph.D.
Rockford, Michigan
jorgensp@gvsu.edu

Chapter 1

Issues in Behavior Modeling

There are two interesting views of a model: as a compromise with reality and as a caricature of reality. Both views are helpful, and both should be kept in mind while reading this book. We build models to improve our understanding of something complex. Architects build models of a proposed building to show a customer what to expect; airplane manufacturers test models in a wind tunnel for flight attributes; and software developers build models of projects they undertake.

1.1 Views of Models

When we think of a model as a compromise with reality, we emphasize that a model cannot describe everything. Think about models of the Earth. It is really a sphere, yet we depict it in two dimensions—shape is lost. Some Earth maps show lines of longitude as perpendicular to lines of latitude. These maps are fine for understanding time zones, and North–South placement, but they exaggerate land area near the poles and reduce it near the equator. In these maps, the Scandinavian peninsula is larger than India, but the reverse is true. Other maps attempt to show proportional land mass, but direction is lost. Model-as-compromise suggests that models have a specific underlying purpose, and that idea is echoed in the following chapters. It will be important to understand that behavioral models cannot (and probably should not) show everything.

Political cartoonists have developed caricature to an art form. World leaders are all instantly recognizable in political cartoons because their dominant features are exaggerated. In the United States as this is being written, caricatures of George W. Bush are generally unflattering, compressing his head, and emphasizing his nose and giving him pointy, elflike ears. At the same time, caricatures show Barack Obama with large ears and a wide smile. Both leaders are easily recognizable. Model-as-caricature is a helpful view of modeling. We hope to use models to emphasize important features of the item being modeled, thereby increasing our understanding and, likely, communicating this to others.

Modeling, then, is something of an art form: we need to recognize both the compromise and caricature aspects of a potential model. Both are important, and both contribute to the overall utility of a model.

1.2 Models of Software

Imagine a three-dimensional diagram, with the axes labeled "data," "function," and "behavior" (sometimes, "control" is used in place of "behavior"), as seen in Figure 1.1. This three-dimensional space is the one in which most of the requirements specification modeling is done, and these axes are conceptually orthogonal to each other. They certainly represent very distinct approaches to modeling a system. The object-oriented community links data and function together (by encapsulation), and the behavior axis remains as a distinct modeling view. None of these views is sufficient by itself, and good modeling practice often moves freely among

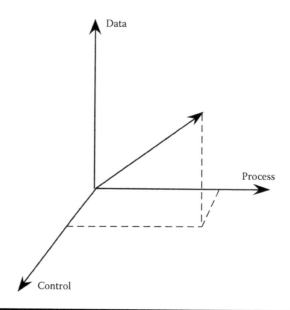

Figure 1.1   Axes in the modeling space.

these three views. To fully understand a system, it must be described in terms of each axis. In this and the following chapters, we are concerned with the behavior axis. This chapter begins to develop a context of the study by discussing some of the issues of requirements analysis. There are other discussions that divide the requirements-specification phase of a project into fine steps: Elicitation, analysis, and specification are the main ones. We are focused on the requirements-analysis portion, specifically, models that describe and explain (and maybe even predict) system behavior.

In the grandfather life-cycle model, the waterfall model, the requirements phase is the foundation of the whole project. This carries over to nearly all of the software development life-cycle models. Indeed, the focus of many of them, for example rapid prototyping and the agile methods, is to get a better understanding of the requirements of a system. We next look at two sets of guidelines for the goals of requirements specification: the traditional one, and a more appropriate modern one. Academics no longer have to sell practitioners on the importance of requirements specification, especially for event-driven systems. Two inescapable forces drive this point home: A large portion of system faults (some say at least half) is due to an inadequate requirements specification, and the cost to resolve a fault found during system testing can be a hundred times the cost of resolving the same error at specification time.

1.2.1 Traditional Goals

Throughout most of the 1970s and 1980s, authors of requirements specification papers exhorted us to produce requirements specifications that are "consistent, complete, and clear," the "3 Cs" that were drilled into software engineering students. The traditional goals of consistency, completeness, and clarity are products of a past time. In the context of traditional applications developed using the waterfall model, they were appropriate. Understanding why they are inappropriate will help show the value of their replacements.

1.2.1.1 Consistency

The demand for consistency is probably an outgrowth of the strong mathematics background of the early software developers. Mathematics (and logic) abhors an inconsistency in much the same way that physics abhors a vacuum. (Everything is true in an inconsistent formal system, thus such systems are of no value.) But what does consistency mean when applied to software? Here are some possibilities:

- The program conforms to its definition.
- The program behaves as expected.
- All representations of the system (requirements specification, design, source and object code) are mutually compatible.

- The program is predictable (deterministic); given the same inputs, it will repeatedly produce the same outputs.
- No two parts of the requirements specification contradict each other.

All of these are desirable, but are they really properties of a requirements specification? The first two are really the goals of developer and customer testing, respectively. The third is the charter of configuration management in the software development process. The fourth view is close, but it really is a program property. Of the possibilities listed here, the fifth comes closest to what "the authors" probably meant when they demanded requirements specification consistency.

Why is (was!) consistency so important? Is it the fear that an inconsistent pair of statements hidden somewhere in the requirements specification may manifest itself someday as an inconsistent pair of system behaviors lurking in the background, waiting for a chance to lend further credence to Murphy's Law? This fear is plausible if software development were sufficiently disciplined so as to implement everything exactly as specified. In most organizations, there is too much "gain" in the development process to make an inconsistency a real problem. The best case to make for this view is transformational implementation (Agresti 1986), in which a system is generated from a very formal specification by a sequence of correctness-preserving transformations. With this paradigm, an inconsistent specification is clearly problematic; however, transformational implementation has had only limited success on very simple applications.

Even if we accept, for the moment, that it really is important to have a consistent requirements specification, how would we ever determine this consistency? Mathematical proofs of consistency are problematic: Kurt Gödel showed that internal-consistency proofs are impossible, and moving to a stronger system to prove that the original is consistent begs the question of the consistency of the stronger system. At the other extreme, human-based techniques such as software reviews don't offer much hope. Practitioners will be forced into a notation-dependent view of consistency. As we shall see, decision tables, for example, have (somewhat relaxed) interpretations of consistency that are, at least, comforting.

1.2.1.2 Completeness

The desire for completeness is much easier to understand, especially in terms of the waterfall model of the software development life cycle. In the waterfall model, if something is missing from the requirements specification, it clearly won't influence the high-level design decisions, and will therefore be absent from both the detailed design and the eventual source code. How embarrassing to deliver a system to a customer and then be told that something obvious (to the customer) is missing. Completeness is certainly desirable, but is it attainable? Once again, the answer depends on what we mean by completeness. Here are some definitions I have collected over the years (the sources are deliberately omitted):

1. No TBD (to be done) sections.
2. All portions required by a given requirements specification standard are present.
3. All referenced items are defined somewhere.
4. All system interfaces are considered.
5. All Ada® packages have a specification part.
6. Notation-dependent forms of completeness.
7. Nothing is missing.

Rather than dwell on all of these, we look at the last two. Typically, with a notation-dependent form of completeness, you know when you're done. But, even if you "are done," have you satisfied the seventh possibility? It refers to problem domain completeness, or semantic completeness; notation-dependent forms of completeness are essentially syntactic, not semantic. The extent to which the syntax of the requirements-specification notation matches the semantics of the application domain is a limiting factor on completeness.

Semantic (maybe "user-defined" is a better term) completeness is the real objective. How attainable is semantic completeness? For well-understood systems, completeness is within reach. These are the ones in which the user and the producer, as a team, have what Agresti (1986) calls "perfect foresight." What happens when we don't have perfect foresight, when neither the user nor the producer fully understands the system being developed? The newer life-cycle models evolved as the practitioner's response. The whole point of rapid prototyping, for example, is to elicit early feedback from the user. For simple systems, experienced developers can derive the behavior from a structural model. For complex systems, rapid prototyping (and its event-driven equivalent, executable specifications) helps us deal with incompleteness. Notice that four of the newer life-cycle paradigms—rapid prototyping, incremental development, evolutionary development, and agile development—all share the premise that the requirements specification is incomplete.

1.2.1.3 Clarity

Of all documents produced during software development, the requirements specification has the widest audience. It is used by the developer, the customer, the independent test team, the maintainer, and by project management. We can also imagine secondary users, such as trainers, installers, repair persons, operators, quality analysts, marketing personnel, and so on. With such a broad audience, no wonder clarity is an issue. Of the three Cs, we should keep clarity. The need for clarity is sometimes at cross purposes with consistency and completeness. Our main conclusion on these is that they are heavily dependent upon the notation used to express the requirements specification. Sadly, notations that help with consistency and completeness are typically too technical to be well understood by the full audience of the requirements specification. Formal specifications can be very unclear. To see this, try to figure out what simple mathematical function, f, is being specified below (Liskov and Berzins 1977).

$$\forall(i, x, y) \ni i, x, \text{ and } y \text{ are integers, } x > 0, y > 0,$$

$$g(f(x, y), x) \wedge g(f(x, y), y) \wedge \forall i \ (g(i, x) \wedge g(i, y) \Rightarrow g(i, f(x, y))),$$

$$\text{where } g(x, y) = \exists\, i \ (y = x * i)$$

More descriptive names are used next; notice that the meaning becomes clear, not because the structure has changed, but because the names give us clues.

For All i, x, and y, where i, x, and y are integers, x > 0, y > 0,

divides(gcd(x, y), x) AND divides(gcd(x, y), y) AND

for all i (divides(i, x) AND divides(i, y) implies divides(i, gcd(x, y))),

where divides(x, y) = exists i (y = x * i)

Be honest—did you recognize this as the specification of the greatest common divisor of two integers? Even worse, did you understand what makes the result maximal? A better way to provide clarity is to consider the information needs of each component in the audience, and then try to produce that information in the requirements specification document. Having all interested parties actively review the document (to defend their own self-interests) is an effective way to ensure that this variety of information needs has been met.

1.2.2 Appropriate Goals

The traditional goals for requirements specification are products of a past time. Major changes since that time obviate the past goals and demand new ones. Consider:

- Size (and its attendant complexity) has increased by orders of magnitude. We now (not routinely) undertake systems on the order of 10 million source lines.
- The waterfall model and its handmaiden, functional decomposition, are challenged by rival life-cycle models and composition.
- Real-time, concurrent, and event-driven systems have inherent complexities that cannot even be represented in traditional notations.

The three goals that I believe are appropriate for requirements specification are responses to the traditional goals that reflect these major changes. Consistency is replaced by executability, completeness by provocation, and clarity by processability.

1.2.2.1 Executability

Nearly all of the models described in Chapters 4 through 9 are executable models, where "executable" means that is possible to write an engine program that executes (or runs) the model. An executable specification (model) acts as a rigorous rapid prototype of a system, and thus provides customer-based feedback. Barry Boehm jokes about the typical customer who says, "I don't know what I want, but I'll recognize it when I see it." Rapid prototyping and executable specifications are two mechanisms to help such customers "experience" the system being proposed.

An avionics company once asked me to attend a presentation by the i-Logix company (later part of Telelogic, and now part of IBM). They were discussing their product, StateMate, which supports the statecharts notation we cover in Chapter 9. One of their success stories was about a model they developed of a ballistic missile launch controller. They worked with the developer to model, with statecharts, a fully-deployed system. To demonstrate the power of their executable specification, they ran an exhaustive execution of the model. The model revealed three sequences of events that would launch a missile. At first, the developers laughed—there were only two known ways to launch a missile. Much to their embarrassment, they finally realized that the (model-identified) third sequence really would launch a missile. Ooops!

David Harel, the creator of the statecharts notation, argues that in the future, most developments will be based on an executable specification (Harel 1988). I suspect this is also true for control-intensive systems.

1.2.2.2 Provocation

Provocation replaces the traditional goal of completeness. Recall that, especially for systems that aren't well understood, completeness simply isn't realistic. Since this clearly applies to event-driven systems, the question becomes how we might improve our system understanding. A model can be provocative in the sense that use of the notation can help us discover aspects of the system that we hadn't thought of. Other disciplines, especially physics, have enjoyed the benefits of provocative notations. Group theory, from mathematics, predicted the existence of subatomic particles before they were observed. Similarly in chemistry, the periodic table of the elements "predicted" elements before they were actually observed. The disciplined use of decision tables, often as a skeleton of an interview technique, forces the consideration of odd combinations that otherwise might easily be ignored. From personal experience, I know of a telephone application that was developed using finite state machines. Although Petri nets would have been a better choice, even the use of finite state machines resulted in the identification of obscure test cases that surprised (and convinced) deeply experienced (and equally skeptical) telephone experts. The people at i-Logix (now IBM) rightfully boasted that, using the statechart notation, they discovered behavior of a missile launching system that the developer hadn't known. A good choice of notation can provide a little "mental momentum" that, in turn, helps with the process of exploring the behavior of systems that are not completely understood.

1.2.2.3 Processability

The traditional goal of clarity maps to processability. Just how processable is a matter of personal (or organizational) taste. Processability comes at a price: The extent of processability depends on the degree of formality in a requirements specification. More formalism implies more effort to develop a requirements specification. Tool developers have created an immense variety of ways to process a requirements specification. Here are a few:

- **Natural-language processors:** The lowest level of processability is clever use of word-processing capabilities. Even this rudimentary view is useful: Some defense contractors use "shall processors" that scan a natural-language document to select and number each sentence that contains the word "shall," which is a keyword in DoD (Department of Defense) requirements. Another successful example is to make consistent changes throughout a large document, especially when synonymous terms must be found and collapsed onto a single chosen standard term.
- **Compiler-oriented processors:** Program Design Languages (PDLs), also known as pseudo-code, have been in use since the mid-1970s. When a requirements specification is written with a PDL, the advantages of structured programming and block structured languages are superimposed onto natural language. The result is a system description that can be processed in compiler-like ways. Some of the forms of completeness cited earlier can be verified with PDL output options, for example, a concordance that shows where items are first defined and where they are used. Since PDLs are based on structured programming languages, they naturally emphasize the structural aspects of a system, thereby providing a strong starting point for development. One last advantage: PDL requirements specifications scale up well for large problems. I once used a PDL requirements specification of a telephone switching system that filled a dozen one-inch three-ring binders. The table of contents was 20 pages long, and the functional decomposition was carefully reflected in the organization.
- **Database approaches:** CASE (computer-aided software engineering) technology, especially those products with active repositories, provides another

distinct form of processability. There are two primary benefits to this form of processability. One is that, with a requirements specification expressed in terms of database structures, we can reduce redundant appearances of information, and ensure consistent use of pieces of information in different system documents. With a requirements specification database, numerous reports and analyses can be devised and derived. The second benefit is that a repository is a fine solution to many of the problems of concurrent development. Problems of networking people working in parallel are reduced to problems of distributed database management, and we've done this for at least a decade.

■ **Executable specifications:** As discussed previously, these are the most important form of requirements specification processability. Thus a processable specification becomes provocative.

1.2.3 Modeling Dichotomies

There are several pairs of words that, when taken together, provide insights into behavioral modeling. Some of these also apply more generally to all of requirements specification.

1.2.3.1 Analysis/Synthesis

Analysis is the process of taking something apart—breaking it into smaller, more comprehensible, and manageable pieces. Synthesis is the opposite: putting things together. Analysis and synthesis are closely related to composition and decomposition, described next. Most engineering disciplines prosper by repeated cycles of analysis followed by synthesis. One of the defects inherent in the waterfall model is that it stresses analysis to the near exclusion of synthesis, resulting in very long feedback cycles between the customer and the developer (Agresti 1986). One of the trends in alternative software development life-cycle models is their emphasis on synthesis. This is best exemplified in the agile development methods, such as extreme programming and test-driven development.

1.2.3.2 Composition/Decomposition

Composition and decomposition are design strategies. Decomposition is a natural activity in analysis, and similarly, composition is part of synthesis. Both strategies have strengths and weaknesses. Decomposition is the most effective way to deal with size. We shall see that finite state machines do not scale up very well, but statecharts (a powerful extension) do, because statecharts effectively deal with size via decomposition. Decomposition, analysis, and top-down development are all tightly associated, and all have been prominent in software development since the 1950s.

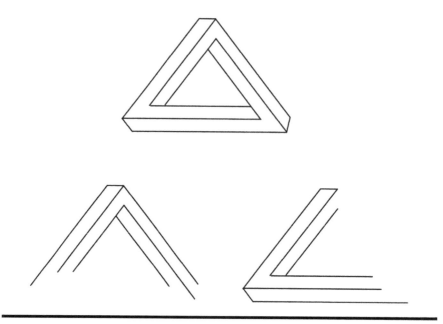

Figure 1.2   M. C. Escher's *Belvedere*.

Composition is more closely associated with synthesis and bottom-up development. The whole object-oriented paradigm centers on reuse, which, in turn, presupposes composition. This pattern was first seen in the iterative versions of waterfall development, and was expanded in object-oriented software development. It seems to have peaked in the agile software development techniques. There will always be a level of uncertainty endemic in composition. Figure 1.2 illustrates this problem in a humorous way: the impossible triangle is composed of two possible corners. The impossibility is actually due to improper composition of the upper and left corners. The upper corner is viewed from the right, while the left corner is viewed from above and slightly left. Notice that, taken by themselves, the corners are normal. The problem occurs when they are composed. For more examples of this, do a Google search on impossible figures or just go to this source: http://www.nationmaster.com/encyclopedia/Penrose-triangle.

1.2.3.3 Prescribed/Proscribed Behavior

Most behavioral models strive to express the prescribed, or intended, behavior of a system. Part of the difficulty of expressing the proscribed (prohibited) behavior is that there are infinitely many things to describe. Lewis Carroll noted this with his "cabbages and kings" phrase. Think about the (obsolete) goal of completeness with respect to proscribed behavior. How could we ever describe all the things that shouldn't happen? We will see that two of our models, decision tables and finite state machines, provide some help with proscribed behavior.

1.2.3.4 Is/Does

The difference between what a system *is* and what a system *does* is seldom considered, yet it is probably the most important. Nearly all of the traditional modeling techniques focus on what the system is. Patterns give an overview of the components of an object-oriented system, and the roles they play. Dataflow diagrams describe the functional decomposition of a system and the (data) interfaces among these components. Class and object models go to great lengths to describe what the system is, including what functional portions must be permanently associated (encapsulated) with which data components. Entity/relationship (E/R) diagrams describe the nature of the major data structures and the various relationships among them. Hierarchy charts add further structural detail to that of dataflow diagrams. Pseudo-code is an extreme example of this; the specification is actually a skeleton of the final source code. There's more to say, but the point should be clear: Most of the common modeling techniques focus on structure—what the system *is*.

This is clearly beneficial to developers. Indeed, adherents of these techniques boast that their favorite notation results in a "seamless transition" from requirements specification through design to source code. If we look more closely, we find that many of the mainline modeling techniques were created by and for developers. Developers are naturally concerned with what a system *is* (*will be* is a better term). After all, it's their job to create it. When they do, they create the components and the interfaces among them so that, when the whole thing executes, it (hopefully) *does* what the customer requested.

History (at least the 40-year history of software development) shows that there are severe limitations to understanding a system in terms of its structure. A few developers can; most customers cannot. The communication gap between customers and developers is enlarged when customers do not understand the implications of models that describe the structure of a system. Have you ever wondered why rapid prototyping is so popular? And effective? It's because rapid prototyping shows the customer what the system *does* (or at least, what it eventually will do). In fact, most customers don't really care about what the system is; but they certainly care about what it does.

The newer modeling techniques describe what a system does. In the mid-1980s, Pamela Zave (1982) was promoting "operational specifications" that only modeled what a system does. Unfortunately, her notation was so close to the Lisp programming language that only programmers fluent in Lisp could understand Pave's PAISLey specification; hardly any customers could. Use cases are widely recognized as an effective way to capture and describe customer requirements. Why? Because they describe scenarios of system behavior. David Harel (1988) predicts that, someday, executable specifications will be the norm, rather than the exception. The growing usage of finite state machines, Petri nets, and statecharts suggests that Harel is right.

If you want to do a good job of requirements specification, you must provide both views. Developers need to understand structure—what it is; and both customers and testers need to understand system behavior—what it does.

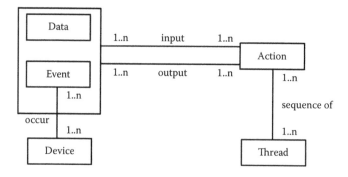

Figure 1.3   Relationships among the fundamental modeling elements.

1.2.4 Fundamental Elements of Modeling

During the 1990s, I was part of a team that developed IEEE Standard 1175, which deals with interfaces among CASE tools. My part of our task was to come up with a set of generic, method-independent concepts that are the basis of all (or most) requirements specification modeling techniques. So far, the terms described next seem to span the mainline models. We shall see how they relate to behavioral models. These fundamental elements are summarized and related to each other by the entity/relationship model in Figure 1.3.

1.2.4.1 Data

When a system is described in terms of its data, the focus is on the information used and created by the system. Data refers to information that is either initialized, stored, updated, or destroyed. For many systems, the data-centered view dominates. These systems are often developed in terms of CRUD actions (create, retrieve, update, delete). We describe data in terms of variables, data structures, fields, records, data stores, and files. Entity/relationship models are the most common choice at the highest level, and some form of a regular expression (e.g., Jackson diagrams or data structure diagrams) is used at a more detailed level. The data-centered view is also the starting point for several flavors of object-oriented analysis.

1.2.4.2 Actions

Action-centered modeling is still a common requirements specification form. This is a historical outgrowth of the action-centered nature of imperative programming languages. Actions have inputs and outputs, and these can be either data or events. Here are some methodology-specific synonyms for actions: transform, data transform, control transform, process, activity, task, method, and service. Actions are typically decomposed into lower level actions.

1.2.4.3 Events

Events are somewhat schizophrenic: They have some characteristics of data and some of actions. An event is a system-level input (or output) that occurs on a port device. Like data, events can be inputs to or outputs of actions. Events can be discrete (such as keystrokes) or they can be continuous (such as temperature, altitude, or pressure). Discrete events necessarily have a time duration, and this can be a critical factor in real-time systems. We might picture input events as destructive read-out data, but it's a stretch to imagine output events as destructive write operations.

Events are like actions in the sense that they are the translation point between real-world physical events and internal logical manifestations of these. Port input events are physical-to-logical translations, and symmetrically, port output events are logical-to-physical translations. System models should focus on the physical side of events, not the logical side. There are situations where the context of present data values changes the logical meaning of physical events. We refer to such situations as "context-sensitive port events." These are very interesting in terms of the expressive power of behavioral models. Similarly, an output event might occur in multiple contexts—a mirror image of context-sensitive input events.

1.2.4.4 Threads

Threads are the least frequently used of the six fundamental constructs. Thread is a dynamic concept; it refers to an end-to-end transaction in an executing system— what a system does. It is easy to find threads in behavioral models, as we will soon see. When an executable model is used, various executions correspond to distinct threads. Threads are of great interest to system testers; indeed, much of a system test case can usually be mechanically derived from a good behavioral model.

1.2.4.5 Devices

Every system has devices; these are the sources and destinations of system-level inputs and outputs (events). Physical actions (keystrokes and light emissions from a screen) occur on devices, and these are translated from physical to logical (or logical to physical). Devices also support the execution of actions. When it is necessary to model concurrency, by definition there must be at least two devices present.

1.2.4.6 Propositions

Propositions, a synonym of conditions, are statements that are either true or false. Most behavioral modeling techniques use propositions to describe conditional situations, for example, an event that has occurred, or a data item that has a certain value. Propositions, together with inherent structure, determine the expressive power of behavioral models. Propositions describe conditions on events, data, actions, and time.

1.2.5 Other Issues

We use models to improve, and maybe to communicate, our understanding of a system. Any model is a compromise with the reality of a system. The expressive power of a model describes how much is lost in the compromise. We end this chapter with a few issues that are germane to the utility of any behavioral model.

1.2.5.1 Size and Complexity

Size and complexity are the primary influencing factors in most models of software development effort estimation. To be useful, behavioral models must be able to deal effectively with size and complexity. Practitioners, especially the skeptical ones, will always ask how well a model can scale up to large, complex systems. These two issues are the primary determinants of the success of a behavioral model.

1.2.5.2 Time

Time is understood, and represented, in several ways: as intervals, as discrete "points" in time, and as an ordering relation (before/after). There are four real-time extensions of the structural analysis: the extension due to Hatley and Pribai (1988), the one by Ward and Mellor (1986), and the merger of these, the Extended Systems Modeling Language (ESML). The fourth is statecharts. Despite their designation as real-time extensions, the first three hardly refer to time. Only the statechart notation has an extensive syntax to express timing considerations. The ability to express time greatly enhances the expressive power of a behavioral model.

1.2.5.3 Concurrency

Concurrency necessarily involves the parallel (in time) execution of at least two devices. President Lyndon B. Johnson used to joke about someone being so dumb they couldn't "walk and chew gum." There is a slight distinction between parallel and concurrent processing. Parallel processing usually refers to several devices working simultaneously and independently. Concurrent processing refers to several devices working simultaneously and interacting (maybe interfering) with each other. Since concurrency involves both devices and time, it is difficult to model well. The statechart notation discussed in Chapter 9 deals explicitly with concurrency.

References

Agresti, William W. 1986. *New paradigms for software development.* Washington, D.C.: IEEE Computer Society Press.

Harel, D. and M. Politi. 1998. *Modeling reactive systems with statecharts: the STATEMATE approach.* New York: McGraw-Hill.

Hatley, Derek J. and I. A. Pirbhai. 1988. *Strategies for Real-Time System Specification*. New York: Dorset House Publishing.

Liskov, B. H. and V. Berzins. 1977. An appraisal of program specifications. In *Proceedings of Research Directions in Software Technology*. Brown University, Providence, R.I.

Ward, Paul T. and Stephen J. Mellor. 1986. *Structured Development for Real-Time Systems*. Upper Saddle River, NJ: Prentice-Hall.

Zave, Pamela. "An operational Approach to Requirements Specification for Embedded Systems," IEEE Transactions on Software Engineering SE-8, May 1982, pp. 250–269.

Exercises

1. Imagine a bar graph for the three axes in Figure 1.1 (data, processing, and control). Plot your estimate of the percentages on each axis for the following applications:
   - Order entry
   - Payroll
   - Numerical integration
   - Hurricane path forecasting
   - An ATM terminal

2. How would you specify the greatest common divisor function in Section 1.1.3?

3. Rapid prototyping is widely acknowledged as an effective way to obtain customer feedback on a proposed system, particularly if the system centers on a GUI (graphical user interface). Discuss this in terms of the executability goal (Section 1.2.1).

4. Look for an M. C. Escher drawing on the Web, e.g., the never-ending staircase or the waterfall. Make a photocopy of it, then see if you can find a point of incorrect interface, as in the impossible triangle example.

5. Develop partial Is and Does views of an automobile. Your Is view might contain subsystems such as the electrical subsystem, the ignition subsystem, and so on. Your Does view should contain scenarios such as starting the engine, braking for a stoplight, and running out of fuel. Then "play" your scenarios against the components in your Is view.

Chapter 2

Math Background

Graph theory is a branch of mathematics that is extraordinarily useful in both modeling and software testing. This chapter summarizes highlights of graph theory and then shows how it is nicely applied in model-based testing. Much of this chapter is taken directly from Jorgensen (2008).

Graph theory is a branch of topology, popularly known as "rubber sheet geometry." This is curious, because the rubber sheet parts of topology have little to do with graph theory; furthermore, the graphs in graph theory do not involve axes, scales, points, and curves, as the name suggests. Whatever the origin of the term, graph theory is probably the most useful part of mathematics for computer science—far more useful than calculus—yet it is not commonly taught. Our excursion into graph theory will follow a "pure math" spirit: Definitions are as devoid of specific interpretations as possible. Postponing interpretations results in maximum latitude in interpretations later, much like well-defined abstract data types promote reuse.

Two basic kinds of graphs are used: undirected and directed. Because the latter is a special case of the former, we begin with undirected graphs. This will allow us to inherit many concepts when we get to directed graphs.

2.1 Graphs

A graph (also known as a linear graph) is an abstract mathematical structure defined from two sets—a set of nodes and a set of edges that form connections between nodes. A computer network is a fine example of a graph. More formally,

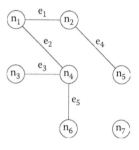

Figure 2.1   A graph with seven nodes and five edges.

Definition

A *graph* $G = (V, E)$ is composed of a finite (and nonempty) set V of nodes and a set E of unordered pairs of nodes, where each edge $e_k = \{n_i, n_j\}$ for some nodes n_i, $n_j \in V$.

The set $\{n_i, n_j\}$ is an unordered pair, which we sometimes write as (n_i, n_j).

Nodes are sometimes called vertices; edges are sometimes called arcs; and we sometimes call nodes the endpoints of an arc. The common visual form of a graph shows nodes as circles and edges as lines connecting pairs of nodes, as in Figure 2.1. We will use this figure as a continuing example, so take a minute to become familiar with it. In the graph in Figure 2.1, the node and edge sets are

$$V = \{n_1, n_2, n_3, n_4, n_5, n_6, n_7\}$$

$$E = \{e_1, e_2, e_3, e_4, e_5\}$$

$$= \{(n_1, n_2), (n_1, n_4), (n_3, n_4), (n_2, n_5), (n_4, n_6)\}$$

To define a particular graph, we must first define a set of nodes and then define a set of edges between pairs of nodes. In many behavioral models, the model elements can be considered, and understood, as nodes in a graph.

2.1.1 Degree of a Node

Definition

The *degree of a node* in a graph is the number of edges that have that node as an endpoint. We write deg(n) for the degree of node n.

We might say that the degree of a node indicates its "popularity" in a graph. In fact, social scientists use graphs to describe social interactions, in which nodes are people and edges often refer to things like "friendship," "communicates with," and so on. The degrees of the nodes in Figure 2.1 are:

$$
\begin{array}{ll}
\deg(n_1) = 2 & \deg(n_5) = 1 \\
\deg(n_2) = 2 & \deg(n_6) = 1 \\
\deg(n_3) = 1 & \deg(n_7) = 0 \\
\deg(n_4) = 3 &
\end{array}
$$

2.1.2 Incidence Matrices

Graphs need not be represented pictorially; they can be fully represented in an incidence matrix, which then can be used to support various mathematical analyses, such as connectivity and reachability.

Definition

The *incidence matrix* of a graph $G = (V, E)$ with m nodes and n edges is an $m \times n$ matrix, where the element in row i, column j is a 1 if and only if node i is an endpoint of edge j; otherwise, the element is 0. The incidence matrix of the graph in Figure 2.1 is in Table 2.1

We can make some observations about a graph by examining its incidence matrix. First, notice that the sum of the entries in any column is 2. That is because every edge has exactly two endpoints. If a column sum in an incidence matrix is ever something other than 2, there is a mistake somewhere. Thus, forming column sums is a form of integrity checking, similar in spirit to that of parity checks. Next, we see that the row sum is the degree of the node. When the degree of a node is

Table 2.1   Incidence Matrix of Figure 2.1

	e_1	e_2	e_3	e_4	e_5
n_1	1	1	0	0	0
n_2	1	0	0	1	0
n_3	0	0	1	0	0
n_4	0	1	1	0	1
n_5	0	0	0	1	0
n_6	0	0	0	0	1
n_7	0	0	0	0	0

zero, as it is for node n_7, we say the node is isolated. This seldom happens in behavioral models.

2.1.3 Adjacency Matrices

The adjacency matrix of a graph is a useful supplement to the incidence matrix. Because adjacency matrices deal with connections, they are the basis of many later graph theory concepts.

Definition

The *adjacency matrix* of a graph $G = (V, E)$ with m nodes is an $m \times m$ matrix, where the element in row i, column j is a 1 if and only if an edge exists between node i and node j; otherwise, the element is 0.

The adjacency matrix is symmetric (element i, j always equals element j, i), and a row sum is the degree of the node (as it was in the incidence matrix). The adjacency matrix of the graph in Figure 2.1 is:

	n_1	n_2	n_3	n_4	n_5	n_6	n_7
n_1	0	1	0	1	0	0	0
n_2	1	0	0	0	1	0	0
n_3	0	0	0	1	0	0	0
n_4	1	0	1	0	0	1	0
n_5	0	1	0	0	0	0	0
n_6	0	0	0	1	0	0	0
n_7	0	0	0	0	0	0	0

2.1.4 Paths

Several behavioral models support the idea of paths—sequences of items in a model. Since most of these models are executable, paths correspond to possible (or impossible!) execution sequences. Paths are one of the main reasons to study graph theory.

Definition

A *path* is a sequence of edges such that, for any adjacent pair of edges e_i, e_j in the sequence, the edges share a common (node) endpoint.

Paths can be described either as sequences of edges or as sequences of nodes; the node sequence choice is more common. Some paths in the graph in Figure 2.1 are:

Path	Node Sequence	Edge Sequence
Between n_1 and n_5	n_1, n_2, n_5	e_1, e_4
Between n_6 and n_5	n_6, n_4, n_1, n_2, n_5	e_5, e_2, e_1, e_4
Between n_3 and n_2	n_3, n_4, n_1, n_2	e_3, e_2, e_1

Paths can be generated directly from the adjacency matrix of a graph using a binary form of matrix multiplication and addition. In our continuing example, edge e_1 is between nodes n_1 and n_2, and edge e_4 is between nodes n_2 and n_5. In the product of the adjacency matrix with itself, the element in position (1, 2) forms a product with the element in position (2, 5), yielding an element in position (1, 5), which corresponds to the two-edge path between n_1 and n_5. If we multiplied the product matrix by the original adjacency matrix again, we would get all three edge paths, and so on.

The graph in Figure 2.1 predisposes a problem. It is not completely general, because it does not show all the situations that might occur in a graph. In particular, no paths exist in which a node occurs twice in the path. If it did, the path would be a loop (or circuit). We could create a circuit by adding an edge between nodes n_3 and n_6.

2.1.5 Connectedness

Paths let us describe and identify nodes that are connected; this leads to a powerful simplification device.

Definition

Nodes n_i and n_j are *connected* if and only if they are in the same path.

Connectedness is an equivalence relation on the node set of a graph. To see this, we can check the three defining properties of equivalence relations:

1. Connectedness is reflexive, because every node is, by default, in a path of length 0 with itself. (Sometimes, for emphasis, an edge is shown that begins and ends on the same node.)
2. Connectedness is symmetric, because if nodes n_i and n_j are in a path, then nodes n_j and n_i are in the same path.
3. Connectedness is transitive, because if nodes n_i and n_j are in a path, and if nodes n_j and n_k are in the same path, then nodes n_i and n_k are in the path,

Equivalence relations induce a partition (a set of disjoint subsets, the union of which is the original set) on a set; therefore, we are guaranteed that connectedness defines a partition on the node set of a graph. This permits the definition of components of a graph:

Definition

A *component of a graph* is a maximal set of connected nodes.

Nodes in the equivalence classes are components of the graph. The classes are maximal due to the transitivity part of the equivalence relation. The graph in Figure 2.1 has two components: $\{n_1, n_2, n_3, n_4, n_5, n_6\}$ and $\{n_7\}$.

2.1.6 Condensation Graphs

We are finally in a position to formalize an important modeling mechanism.

Definition

Given a graph $G = (V, E)$, its *condensation graph* is formed by replacing each component by a condensing node.

Developing the condensation graph of a given graph is an unambiguous (i.e., algorithmic) process. We use the adjacency matrix to identify path connectivity, and then use the equivalence relation to identify components. The absolute nature of this process is important: The condensation graph of a given graph is unique. This implies that the resulting simplification represents an important aspect of the original graph.

The components in our continuing example are $S_1 = \{n_1, n_2, n_3, n_4, n_5, n_6\}$ and $S_2 = \{n_7\}$.

No edges can be present in a condensation graph of an ordinary (undirected) graph. Two reasons are:

1. Edges have individual nodes as endpoints, not sets of nodes.
2. Even if we fudge the definition of edge to ignore this distinction, a possible edge would mean that nodes from two different components were connected, thus in a path, thus in the same (maximal!) component.

2.1.7 Cyclomatic Number

Cyclomatic complexity is another property of graphs that has deep implications for the inherent complexity of a model.

Definition

The *cyclomatic number* of a graph G is given by $V(G) = e - n + p$, where

    e is the number of edges in G
    n is the number of nodes in G
    p is the number of components in G

$V(G)$ is the number of distinct regions in a strongly connected directed graph, which we discuss next.

2.2 Directed Graphs

Directed graphs are a slight refinement to ordinary graphs: Edges acquire a sense of direction. Symbolically, the unordered pairs (n_i, n_j) become ordered pairs $<n_i, n_j>$, and we speak of a directed edge going from node n_i to n_j, instead of being between the nodes.

Definition

A *directed graph* (or digraph) $D = (V, E)$ consists of: a finite set $V = \{n_1, n_2, ..., n_m\}$ of nodes and a set $E = \{e_1, e_2, ..., e_p\}$ of edges, where each edge $e_k = <n_i, n_j>$ is an ordered pair of nodes $n_i, n_j \in V$.

    In the directed edge $e_k = <n_i, n_j>$, n_i is the initial (or start) node, and n_j is the terminal (or finish) node. Edges in directed graphs fit naturally with many software concepts: sequential behavior, imperative programming languages, time-ordered events, define/reference pairings, messages, function and procedure calls, and so on. The difference between ordinary and directed graphs is very analogous to the difference between declarative and imperative programming languages. In imperative languages (e.g., COBOL, FORTRAN, Pascal, C, Java, Ada®), the sequential order of source language statements determines the execution time order of compiled code. Decision tables (Chapter 5) are declarative; most other behavioral models are imperative.

    The next series of definitions roughly parallels the ones for ordinary graphs. We modify our now-familiar continuing example to the one shown in Figure 2.2. We have the same node set $V = \{n_1, n_2, n_3, n_4, n_5, n_6, n_7\}$, and the edge set appears to be the same: $E = \{e_1, e_2, e_3, e_4, e_5\}$. The difference is that the edges are now ordered pairs of nodes in V:

$$E = \{<n_1, n_2>, <n_1, n_4>, <n_3, n_4>, <n_2, n_5>, <n_4, n_6>\}$$

2.2.1 Indegrees and Outdegrees

The degree of a node in an ordinary graph is refined to reflect direction, as follows:

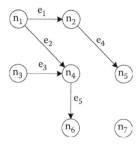

Figure 2.2   A directed graph.

Definition

The *indegree of a node* in a directed graph is the number of distinct edges that have the node as a terminal node. We write indeg(n) for the indegree of node n.

The *outdegree of a node* in a directed graph is the number of distinct edges that have the node as a start point. We write outdeg(n) for the outdegree of node n.

The nodes in the digraph in Figure 2.2 have the following indegrees and outdegrees:

$$\begin{aligned}
\text{indeg}(n_1) &= 0 & \text{outdeg}(n_1) &= 2 \\
\text{indeg}(n_2) &= 1 & \text{outdeg}(n_2) &= 1 \\
\text{indeg}(n_3) &= 0 & \text{outdeg}(n_3) &= 1 \\
\text{indeg}(n_4) &= 2 & \text{outdeg}(n_4) &= 1 \\
\text{indeg}(n_5) &= 1 & \text{outdeg}(n_5) &= 0 \\
\text{indeg}(n_6) &= 1 & \text{outdeg}(n_6) &= 0 \\
\text{indeg}(n_7) &= 0 & \text{outdeg}(n_7) &= 0
\end{aligned}$$

Ordinary and directed graphs meet through definitions that relate obvious correspondences, such as: $\text{deg}(n) = \text{indeg}(n) + \text{outdeg}(n)$.

2.2.2 Types of Nodes

The added descriptive power of directed graphs lets us define different kinds of nodes:

Definition

A node with indegree = 0 is a *source node*.
A node with outdegree = 0 is a *sink node*.
A node with indegree ≠ 0 and outdegree ≠ 0 is a *transfer node*.

Source and sink nodes constitute the external boundary of a graph. If we made a directed graph of a context diagram (from a set of dataflow diagrams produced by structured analysis), the external entities would be source and sink nodes.

In our continuing example, n_1, n_3, and n_7 are source nodes; n_5, n_6, and n_7 are sink nodes; and n_2 and n_4 are transfer (also known as interior) nodes. A node that is both a source and a sink node is an isolated node. Node n_7 in Figure 2.2 is an isolated node.

2.2.3 Adjacency Matrix of a Directed Graph

As we might expect, the addition of direction to edges changes the definition of the adjacency matrix of a directed graph.

Definition

The *adjacency matrix of a directed graph* D = (V, E) with m nodes is an m × m matrix: $A = (a_{i,j})$, where $a_{i,j}$ is a 1 if and only if there is an edge from node i to node j; otherwise, the element is 0.

The adjacency matrix of a directed graph is not necessarily symmetric. A row sum is the outdegree of the node; a column sum is the indegree of a node. The adjacency matrix of our continuing example is:

	n_1	n_2	n_3	n_4	n_5	n_6	n_7
n_1	0	1	0	1	0	0	0
n_2	0	0	0	0	1	0	0
n_3	0	0	0	1	0	0	0
n_4	0	0	0	0	0	1	0
n_5	0	0	0	0	0	0	0
n_6	0	0	0	0	0	0	0
n_7	0	0	0	0	0	0	0

One common use of directed graphs is to record family relationships, in which siblings, cousins, and so on are connected by an ancestor; and parents, grandparents, and so on are connected by a descendant. Entries in powers of the adjacency matrix now show existence of directed paths.

2.2.4 Paths and Semipaths

Direction permits a more precise meaning to paths that connect nodes in a directed graph. As a handy analogy, you may think in terms of one-way and two-way streets.

Definition

A (directed) *path* is a sequence of edges such that, for any adjacent pair of edges e_i, e_j in the sequence, the terminal node of the first edge is the initial node of the second edge.

A *cycle* is a directed path that begins and ends at the same node.

A (directed) *semipath* is a sequence of edges such that, for at least one adjacent pair of edges e_i, e_j in the sequence, the initial node of the first edge is the initial node of the second edge or the terminal node of the first edge is the terminal node of the second edge.

Directed paths are sometimes called chains; we will use this concept in Chapter 9. Our continuing example contains the following paths and semipaths (not all are listed):

A path from n_1 to n_6
A semipath between n_1 and n_3
A semipath between n_2 and n_4
A semipath between n_5 and n_6

2.2.5 Reachability Matrix

When we model an application with a digraph, we often ask questions that deal with paths that let us reach (or "get to") certain nodes. This is an extremely useful capability and is made possible by the reachability matrix of a digraph.

Definition

The *reachability matrix* of a directed graph $D = (V, E)$ with m nodes is an m × m matrix $R = (r_{i,j})$, where $r_{i,j}$ is a 1 if and only if there is a path from node i to node j; otherwise the element is 0.

The reachability matrix of a directed graph D can be calculated from the adjacency matrix A as follows:

$$R = I + A + A^2 + A^3 + \ldots + A^k$$

where k is the length of the longest path in D, and binary addition is defined to be $(1 + 1 = 1)$. The reachability matrix for our continuing example is:

	n_1	n_2	n_3	n_4	n_5	n_6	n_7
n_1	1	1	0	1	1	1	0
n_2	0	1	0	0	1	0	0
n_3	0	0	1	1	0	1	0
n_4	0	0	0	1	0	1	0
n_5	0	0	0	0	1	0	0
n_6	0	0	0	0	0	1	0
n_7	0	0	0	0	0	0	1

The reachability matrix tells us that nodes n_2, n_4, n_5, and n_6 can be reached from n_1, node n_5 can be reached from n_2, and so on. This will be important in finite state machines (Chapter 6).

2.2.6 n-Connectedness

Connectedness of ordinary graphs extends to a rich, highly explanatory concept for digraphs.

Definition

Two nodes n_i and n_j in a directed graph are:

0-connected iff (if and only if) no path exists between n_i and n_j
1-connected iff a semipath but no path exists between n_i and n_j
2-connected iff a path exists between n_i and n_j
3-connected iff a path goes from n_i to n_j and a path goes from n_j to n_i

No other degrees of connectedness exist.

We need to modify our continuing example to show 3-connectedness (see Figure 2.3). The change is the addition of a new edge e_6 from n_6 to n_3, so the graph

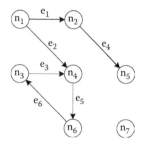

Figure 2.3   Revision of the directed graph in Figure 2.2.

contains a cycle. With this change, we have the following instances of n-connectivity in Figure 2.3 (not all are listed):

n_1 and n_7 are 0-connected
n_2 and n_6 are 1-connected
n_1 and n_6 are 2-connected
n_3 and n_6 are 3-connected

In terms of one-way streets, you cannot get from n_2 to n_6.

2.2.7 Strong Components

The analogy continues. We get two equivalence relations from n-connectedness: 1-connectedness yields what we might call "weak connection," and this in turn yields weak components. (These turn out to be the same as we had for ordinary graphs, which is what should happen, because 1-connectedness effectively ignores direction.) The second equivalence relation, based on 3-connectedness, is more interesting. As before, the equivalence relation induces a partition on the node set of a digraph, but the condensation graph is quite different. Nodes that previously were 0-, 1-, or 2-connected remain so. The 3-connected nodes become the strong components.

Definition

A *strong component of a directed graph* is a maximal set of 3-connected nodes.

In our amended example, the strong components are the sets $\{n_3, n_4, n_6\}$ and $\{n_7\}$. The condensation graph for our amended example is shown in Figure 2.4.

Strong components let us simplify by removing loops and isolated nodes. Notice that the condensation graph of a digraph will never contain a loop. (If it did, the loop would have been condensed by the maximal aspect of the partition.) These graphs have a special name: directed acyclic graphs, sometimes written as DAG.

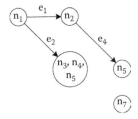

Figure 2.4   Condensation graph of Figure 2.3.

2.3 Model-Based Testing

Model-based testing entails the derivation of test cases from some model that describes the software being tested. Usually, test cases correspond to paths in a directed graph that underlies a modeling technique. (For a complete treatment, see [Utting 2007].) Most of the models discussed in this book—namely finite state machines, ordinary Petri nets, event-driven Petri nets, and statecharts—have a strong basis in graph theory. From the respective graph theory descriptions, we are able to identify paths, hence test cases. One of the clear advantages of model-based testing is that the generated test cases can obviously be traced back to the specification, so various forms of model-based test coverage can be postulated. We can stretch derivation of test cases to rules in a decision table, leaving flowcharts (Chapter 4) as the only model discussed here that does not support model-based testing.

An execution engine is a program that is capable of simulating the execution of a model. When a model is executed by its corresponding engine, the result is the automatic identification of paths in the model, and these correspond to test cases. Depending on the formality of the underlying model, the corresponding execution engines have varying degrees of power. Some engines, for example those for finite state machines, can only be executed by having a user interact with a model, thereby directing the execution. This is useful in itself, because executing the model acts like a rapid prototype (that supports the *does* view, as discussed in Chapter 1). At the other extreme, the execution engine for statecharts supports seven levels of increasingly intensive execution. As the various models are described in the remaining chapters, there will always be a section at the end of a chapter describing how an engine might execute the model.

References

Jorgensen, P. C. 2008. *Software testing: A craftsman's approach*. 3rd ed. New York: Taylor and Francis.

Utting, Mark, and Bruno Legard. 2007. *Practical model-based testing: A tools approach*. San Francisco: Morgan Kaufman.

Exercises

1. In the adjacency matrix of an undirected graph, is the column sum of node i always equal to the row sum of node i? Why, or why not?
2. How might you define the length of a path in an undirected graph? Would your definition be any different for paths in a directed graph? What if there is a loop (or a three-connected component of a directed graph)?
3. The text says: "The classes are maximal due to the transitivity part of the equivalence relation." Explain this in your own words.
4. Can you think of meanings for column sums and row sums in the adjacency matrix of a directed graph?
5. Social scientists sometimes use directed graphs to describe social situations. Define a graph in which nodes are people, and there is an edge from node i to node j if (and only if) person i speaks with person j. Now how might you interpret
   - a node with high indegree?
   - a node with high outdegree?
   - a strong component?

Chapter 3

Examples

Well-chosen examples are helpful in understanding the issues of behavior modeling. We begin with mainline issues, and then describe the examples and notation that are used in the subsequent chapters. Five of the examples will be done in every chapter; the others are left for student/reader practice.

3.1 Issues in Behavior Modeling

The issues of behavior modeling center on three main topics: the constructs of structured programming, task management, and events. There is a mapping of these issues to our examples at the end of this chapter.

3.1.1 Structured Programming Constructs

The precepts of structured programming were introduced in the early 1970s as a way of simplifying "spaghetti code," which got its name from the way programmers marked up source code listings to follow program execution sequences. In 1966, Bohm and Jacopini proved that any program could be written with three simple structures: sequence, selection, and repetition (Bohm 1966). By eliminating the infamous GoTo and, worse, the Computed Go To statements, program control complexity (aka cyclomatic, or McCabe, complexity) is greatly reduced. In most imperative programming languages, selection is expanded into three forms: If,Then; If,Then,Else; and the Case (or Switch) statements. Similarly, repetition takes on three common forms: precondition (While), postcondition (Until), and computed (For) program loops. While familiarity with these is assumed here, it is worth noting that, ultimately, all of the "higher order" behavioral issues must be reduced to these when a behavioral model is implemented in source code.

3.1.2 Task Management

While the structured programming constructs addressed control issues at the programming-in-the-small level, the programming-in-the-large community was dealing with controlling tasks. The practitioner community developed three main "real-time extensions" to the dominant modeling technique—structured analysis. Frustrated by the difficulty of modeling avionics and process-control systems with ordinary dataflow diagrams, Derek Hatley and Imtiaz Pirbhai (1988), Paul Ward (1986), and others developed modeling extensions to express control relationships among tasks. These were somewhat standardized in the Extended Systems Modeling Language (ESML) promoted by an ad hoc industrial group. They identified seven primary task-control primitives, called ESML prompts, defined next.

Definition

Let A be a *task* that controls task B. Then

Task A *enables* task B when the execution of task A makes it possible for task B to execute.

Task A *disables* task B when the execution of task A makes it impossible for task B to execute.

Task A *triggers* task B when the execution of task A causes task B to execute immediately.

Task A *activates* task B when the execution of task A first enables and later disables task B.

Task A *suspends* task B when the execution of task A terminates the execution of task B.

Task A *resumes* task B when the execution of task A triggers the execution of task B at the point at which it was suspended.

Task A *pauses* task B when the execution of task A suspends and later resumes task B.

These ESML task-controlling primitives should not be confused with actions that cause output events. This is a fine distinction: In a finite state machine model (see Chapter 6), state transitions may have associated output events. In one sense, these events are caused by a software task executing. In Chapters 8 and 9, we will see that Petri net formulations clarify this distinction.

In parallel with the real-time extension activity, the operating system and Petri net communities took a higher level view of task control.

Definition

Let *tasks* A and B be two tasks that can potentially execute simultaneously. (They are "enabled" in the ESML sense.) Then

Prioritization occurs when the model ensures that task A executes before task B. (This often takes the form of an interlock.)

Mutual exclusion occurs when the model ensures that tasks A and B cannot execute simultaneously.

Parallel execution occurs when the model ensures that tasks A and B execute simultaneously.

Deadlock occurs when no task is enabled (again in the ESML sense).

The community of computer science theorists explored two other, task-related notions: nontermination and nondeterminism. Nontermination can be of the esoteric Halting Problem form, or it can be as simple as infinite program loops. One form of nondeterminism occurs when the output of a program (or model) is not a function of its inputs. The other, more interesting form of nondeterminism occurs in behavioral models. This form is almost always related to inconsistency.

3.1.3 Events

There are two views of an event: as a physical action performed by a program user or as the (usually software-based) recognition of a physical event. Testers and program users tend to take the first view, and software developers usually take the second view. Events are either inputs or outputs, and they are visible to the tester/program user. Since event-driven systems have become so common, we identify four issues related to events in this subsection.

3.1.3.1 Context-Sensitive Input Events

Context-sensitive input events are physical events that have different logical meanings, depending on the "context" in which they occur. When a telephone customer picks up a handset, for example, that is a physical event known as Go Off Hook in telephony parlance. There are half a dozen logical meanings to Go Off Hook, and each determines a distinct telephone response. If Go Off Hook occurs when the line is idle, it is interpreted as "call origination" and dial tone is provided. If Go Off Hook occurs when the line is ringing, it is interpreted as "call answer," and a talk path is provided. If a system has context-sensitive input events, it is obviously necessary to identify all the potential contexts of these events in a behavioral model.

3.1.3.2 Multiple-Context Output Events

There is a symmetric, and more subtle, problem for output events. Consider a system in which there are multiple causes of a particular output event. If the only thing observed is the output event, there is no (easy) way to determine its cause. This problem is usually recognized during the maintenance phase of a software product, in which field trouble reports may be incomplete, only mentioning an unexpected output and not providing enough other information to identify the thread that caused the event. When a system has the potential for these ambiguous output events, the behavioral model should support the identification of all threads that include the ambiguous event among its output events.

3.1.3.3 Discrete and Continuous Events

Both input and output events can be either discrete or continuous. A discrete event has a short, possibly infinitesimal, duration. The lever and dial actions in the Saturn Windshield Wiper example (see Section 3.2.5) are discrete input events, and the various wiper speed outputs are understood as continuous.

3.1.3.4 Event Orders

The final issue regarding events is event order. In a character-based user interface (CUI), it is customary for program prompts to determine the sequence of input events. This is no longer true in a graphical user interface (GUI), where input events can occur in any order. David Harel (1998) refers to such systems as "reactive," in the sense that they react to their inputs. A behavioral model of a reactive system should express, or at least tolerate, any order of input events, and these are usually called asynchronous events. If concurrent execution is possible, there is the possibility of simultaneous events, and this requires a very expressive behavioral model. One of the characteristics of event-driven systems is the possibility that no event occurs. Such points are known as event quiescence, and these are similar, but not identical, to deadlock.

3.2 Continuing Examples

3.2.1 Simplified U.S. 1040EZ Income Tax Form

We make two simplifications to the U.S. 1040EZ tax form: Earned Income Credit is taken as an input, and a function (TaxTable) is substituted for the four pages of tax tables. There are only five inputs to form U.S. 1040EZ; they are: Wages, Taxable interest, unEmploymentCompensation, marital status (single or married), and a Boolean variable that describes whether or not the filer can be claimed as a dependent on somebody else's income tax. (The constants used here are from the tax year 2007 instructions.) The following quantities must be computed: AdjustedGrossIncome, minimumStandardDeduction, maximum-StandardDeduction, StandardDeduction, and taxableIncome. The computations are as follows:

AdjustedGrossIncome = Wages + taxableInterest + unEmploymentCompensation
minStandardDeduction = Max($850, (Wages + $300))
If single, then maxStandardDeduction = $5380
If married, then maxStandardDeduction = $10700
StandardDeduction = min(minStandardDeduction, maxStandardDeduction)
taxableIncome = AdjGrossIncome − StandardDeduction
tax = TaxTable(AdjGrossIncome)

Input Variable	Description	Computed Variable	Description
W	Wages	AGI	AdjustedGrossIncome
txInt	Taxable interest	minStDed	minimumStandardDeduction
unEmpComp	unEmployment-Compensation	maxStDed	maximumStandardDeduction
marStat	Marital status	StDed	StandardDeduction
		taxInc	taxableIncome
		tax	tax

Table 3.1 lists the behavioral issues and selected examples in the Simplified U.S. 1040EZ Income Tax Form problem.

Table 3.1 Behavioral Issues in U.S. 1040EZ

Issue	Example
Sequence	• Getting input values before using them • Using results of decisions in computations
Selection	• Decisions based on marital status

Table 3.2 Behavioral Issues in NextDate

Issue	Example
Sequence	• Validating input value ranges before validating date • Validating date before incrementing it
Selection	• Many: validating data ranges, determining leap years

3.2.2 The NextDate Function

Because of the interesting logical dependencies among its input variables, the NextDate function is popular in software testing circles. NextDate is a function of three variables—month, day, and year. On execution, it returns the month, day, and year of the next day. The variables are all bounded, positive integers.

$1 <= $ month $<= 12$
$1 <= $ day $<= 31$
$1812 <= $ year $<= 2012$

Table 3.2 lists the behavioral issues and selected examples in the NextDate problem.

3.2.3 Espresso Vending Machine

3.2.3.1 Espresso Vending Machine (Full Version)

An espresso costs €1 (one Euro). (Sorry, no cream, no sugar.) A coin-return button can be pressed at any time BEFORE a total of €1 has been deposited. Espresso is dispensed automatically once at least €1 has been deposited.

Port input events
  e1. Insert €1 coin
  e2. Insert €0.20 coin
  e3. Insert €0.50 coin
  e4. (request) Return all coins

Port output events (actions)
  a1. (no action)
  a2. Dispense espresso
  a3 Return coins

Table 3.3 Behavioral Issues in the Espresso Vending Machine

Issue	*Example*
Sequence	• Sequences of coin insertion events • Payment before dispensing espresso
Selection	• Recognizing need for more coins
Repetition	• Building total value of coins
Disable	• Coin return request
Context-sensitive input events	• Coin insertions—no dispense until total is reached
Multiple-context output events	• Espresso dispense can occur after any of three different coins is inserted
Asynchronous events	• Coins can be inserted at any time
Event quiescence	• Must wait for next coin when total is less than €1.00

Table 3.3 lists the behavioral issues and selected examples in the Espresso Vending Machine.

3.2.3.2 Espresso Vending Machine (Six-Coin Version)

In this simplified version, the espresso customer has exactly six coins: a €0.50 coin and five €0.10 coins. The coins can be inserted in any order, but all coins must be used.

Port input events
 e1. Insert €0.50 coin
 e2. Insert €0.10 coin

Port output events (Actions)
 a1. (no action)
 a2. Dispense espresso
 a3. Return coins

3.2.4 Smart Fuel Pump

The Smart Fuel Pump (SFP) System combines computer technology with traditional gas station equipment. This is an extension of a problem used by Derek Coleman (Coleman 1994). The SFP System supports fuel-pumping devices with two interfaces: one for the customer, and the other for the station attendant.

The fuel pump nozzle, trigger, and holster are only mildly changed from the familiar, strictly manual devices. When the nozzle is removed from the holster and inserted into the fuel tank, squeezing the trigger starts the flow of fuel. Releasing the trigger stops the flow. The trigger can be squeezed and released several times. Fuel delivery is ended when the nozzle is replaced in the holster. Whenever fuel is flowing out of the nozzle, the displays on the Customer Interface and the Attendant Interface are being updated. Each fuel tank has a level sensor. If the fuel level ever drops below the 4% mark, fuel delivery is immediately terminated.

The Customer Interface supports several capabilities:

- Selection of fuel grade (three grades of unleaded gasoline: regular, mid-grade, and premium)
- Continuous display of quantity of fuel delivered and price of amount of fuel delivered. Fuel volume is measured in gallons and thousandths of a gallon. Transaction price is measured in dollars and thousandths of a dollar.
- Static display of cost of each grade of fuel
- Selection of payment mode (pay inside or credit card)

There is a small, character-only display screen (ten lines of up to 40 characters).

The Attendant Interface has the following capabilities:

- Display of individual pump status (idle, enabled, in use, delivery complete)
- Display of amount and price of fuel being delivered (per pump)
- Means to enable and disable individual pumps
- Means to change the price of grades of fuel

In addition, there is a Credit Card Subsystem embedded into each Smart Fuel Pump. Though not technically part of the Smart Fuel Pump System, the Credit Card Subsystem has an interface with the enabling and disabling mechanisms. It also captures the transaction quantities (volume and price) and forwards these to the credit card company, along with station-specific information, such as the station name, identification number, transaction date, and so on.

In normal operation, a customer parks his or her vehicle close to a Smart Fuel Pump, removes the fuel tank cover, and begins a transaction by

- selecting a payment method,
- selecting a fuel grade, and
- removing the nozzle from the holster and placing it in the tank opening.

Table 3.4 Behavioral Issues in the Smart Fuel Pump

Issue	*Example*
Sequence	• Transaction approval before making fuel selection • Nozzle removal before trigger squeeze
Selection	• Fuel grade selection
Repetition	• Trigger squeeze and release
Enable	• Transaction approval enables pump • Nonoccurrence of the 4% level event
Disable	• Transaction rejection disables pump • 4% level event disables most of system
Trigger	• Trigger squeeze triggers display updates
Activate	• Nozzle removal activates trigger, display functions
Suspend	• Trigger release during pumping
Resume	• Trigger squeeze after a trigger release
Pause	• Trigger squeeze and release; display resumes where it left off
Mutual exclusion	• Fuel type selection
Concurrent execution	• Pumping, displays, tank level sensing
Multiple-context output events	• Starting the pump
Asynchronous events	• Nozzle, trigger, and 4% level events
Event quiescence	• After trigger release • Before fuel grade selection

If the customer selects the "pay inside" option, the attendant must enable the pump. (The "pay inside" option causes a "pump enable request" lamp to be lit on the attendant console.) The attendant can either enable the pump, or, if the customer is suspicious, cause a "pay in advance" message to be displayed on the customer message screen.

If the customer selects the credit card payment option, the pump enabling process is triggered by the approval signal from the Credit Card Subsystem. (If credit is denied, an appropriate message appears on the customer screen.) When a customer completes fuel delivery, replacement of the nozzle into the holster causes a packet of data to be transmitted either to the credit card company or to the attendant. Table 3.4 lists the behavioral issues and selected examples in the Smart Fuel Pump problem.

3.2.5 *Saturn Windshield Wiper Controller*

The windshield wiper on older Saturn automobiles is controlled by a lever with a dial on its end. The lever has four positions, OFF, INT (for intermittent), LOW, and HIGH, and the dial has three positions, numbered simply 1, 2, and 3. The dial positions indicate three intermittent speeds, and the dial position is relevant only when the lever is at the INT position. The table below shows the windshield wiper speeds (in wipes per minute) for the lever and dial positions.

c1.	Lever	OFF	INT	INT	INT	LOW	HIGH
c2.	Dial	n/a	1	2	3	n/a	n/a
a1.	Wiper	0	6	12	20	30	60

Table 3.5 lists the behavioral issues and selected examples in the Saturn Windshield Wiper Controller problem.

We will use this problem to illustrate execution tables in Chapters 6 (Finite State Machines), 8 (Event-Driven Petri Nets), and 9 (Statecharts). Each execution table will refer to the following use case:

Table 3.5   Behavioral Issues in the Saturn Windshield Wiper

Issue	*Example*
Sequence	• Lever up and down events
	• Dial up and down events
Selection	• …
Repetition	• Next event loop in flowchart
Enable	• Intermittent lever position enables the dial
Disable	• Leaving the intermittent lever position disables the dial • Entering the Lever Off position disables the wiper
Context-sensitive input events	• Lever events • Dial events
Asynchronous events	• Lever and dial events can occur in any order
Event quiescence	• Occurs in every lever position

Use Case Name:	Saturn Windshield Wiper Controller execution table example	
Use Case ID:	SWWC-1	
Description:	Operator moves through a typical sequence of lever and dial events	
Preconditions:	1. Lever position is OFF, Dial position is 1	
Event Sequence:	*Input Event*	*System Response*
	1. e1: move lever up one position	2. a2: deliver 6 wipes per minute
	3. e3: move dial up one position	4. a3: deliver 12 wipes per minute
	5. e1: move lever up one position	6. a5: deliver 12 wipes per minute
	7. e1: move lever up one position	8. a6: deliver 12 wipes per minute
	9. e2: move lever down one position	10. a5: deliver 12 wipes per minute
	11. e3: move dial up one position	…
	12. e2: move lever down one position	13. a4: deliver 20 wipes per minute
	14. e2: move lever down one position	15. a1: deliver 0 wipes per minute
Postconditions:	1. Lever position is OFF, Dial position is 3	

3.3 Examples for Readers

3.3.1 Windchill Factor Table

The famous (in Michigan and other cold parts of the United States) windchill factor (W) is a function of two variables: wind speed in miles per hour (V) and temperature in Fahrenheit degrees (T). The actual formula is:

$$W = 35.74 + 0.6215*T - 35.75*(V^{0.16}) + 0.4275*T*(V^{0.16})$$

where W is the apparent temperature on a human face, measured in degrees Fahrenheit; T is the air temperature, measured in degrees Fahrenheit, –20 <= T

<= 50; and V is the wind velocity measured in miles per hour, 3 <= V <= 73. (The ranges are arbitrary, but also realistic for Michigan!)

Build a windchill table for temperatures in the –20 <= T <= 50 range at 5 degree increments, and wind speeds in the 3 <= V <= 73 range at 5 mph increments.

3.3.2 The Previous Date Function

The Previous Date function is the inverse of the NextDate function. It is also a function of three variables: month, day, and year. Upon execution, it returns the month, day, and year of the previous day. The variables are all bounded, positive integers.

> 1 <= month <= 12
> 1 <= day <= 31
> 1812 <= year <= 2012

3.3.3 Saturn Cruise Control

The user controls for the cruise control system on a 2002 Saturn are mounted on the steering wheel. On the left side, there is a button labeled "Cruise On/Off," and it contains a tiny lamp that is lit when the cruise control mechanism in On. The Cruise On/Off button is a toggle. The other button (on the right side of the steering wheel) is more complex; it is actually two buttons, and events are time dependent. It has the labels "Res/AcceL" and "Set/Coast." The cruise control mechanism maintains a (fairly) constant automobile speed at speeds above 25 mph, and it obviates the driver's need to maintain pressure on the accelerator pedal. The following operating instructions are paraphrased from the Saturn owner's manual.

1. To set cruise control, press the Cruise On/Off button. The lamp will be lit. Bring the car to the desired speed (greater than 25 mph) and press the Set/Coast button. At this point, the driver may remove his foot from the accelerator pedal.
2. There are two ways to disable the cruise control mechanism: step on the brake pedal or press the Cruise On/Off button. After either event, the lamp will no longer be lit, and the cruise control mechanism is disabled.
3. If the cruise control mechanism was disabled by applying the brake, and if the car is moving at a speed at or above 25 mph, pressing the Res/AcceL button will enable the cruise control mechanism at the previously set speed.
4. There are three ways to increase the speed while the cruise control mechanism is active:
   - Use the accelerator pedal to bring the car to a higher speed and then press the Set/Coast button.
   - Press and hold the Res/AcceL button until the car reaches the desired speed and then release the Res/AcceL button.

- Depress the Res/AcceL button for less than a half second, which increments the speed by 1 mph.
5. There are two ways to decrease the speed while the cruise control mechanism is active:
   - Press and hold the Set/Coast button until the car reaches the desired speed and then release the Set/Coast button.
   - Depress the Set/Coast button for less than a half second, which decrements the speed by 1 mph.

Input events
  p1. Touch Cruise On/Off
  p2. Touch Set/Coast
  p3. Hold Set/Coast for less than 0.5 seconds
  p4. Hold Set/Coast for more than 0.5 seconds
  p5. Touch Res/AcceL
  p6. Hold Res/AcceL for less than 0.5 seconds
  p7. Hold Res/AcceL for more than 0.5 seconds
  p8. Touch brake pedal
  p9. Driver accelerate to desired speed
  p10. Driver decelerate to desired speed
  p11. Driver release accelerator pedal

Output events
  p12. Cruise control lamp ON
  p13. Cruise control lamp OFF
  p14. Maintain present speed
  p15. Increase present speed by 1 mph
  p16. Decrease present speed by 1 mph
  p17. Continually increase present speed
  p18. Continually decrease present speed

Data places
  d1. Desired speed
  d2. Actual speed
  d3. Cruise Control OFF
  d4. Cruise Control ON, Active
  d5. Cruise Control ON, passive

3.3.4 Programmable Thermostat

The programmable thermostat has three operating modes: Off, Heating, and Cooling. These are selected by touches on the "Mode" button, which cycles through the three modes. There is a temperature-display device that displays either the ambient or the desired temperature (see Figure 3.1). This device defaults to the ambient temperature, and it responds to touches on the temperature-control arrow buttons. Pressing either the Up or Down button first shows the desired temperature, and successive touches on these buttons raise/lower the desired temperature by one degree (Fahrenheit).

There is a constantly available input of the ambient temperature, and this is displayed continuously, except when the temperature-control buttons are active.

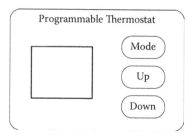

Figure 3.1   Programmable thermostat user interface.

When the system is not in the Off mode, the device constantly compares the desired and ambient temperatures. When there is a difference of two degrees, the system activates the furnace or the air conditioner, depending on which mode is active. Ambient temperature "overshoots" are ignored. For example, if the system is in the heating mode and the ambient temperature is greater than the desired temperature, no action is taken.

The port devices are: Mode button, Temperature display, Up button, Down button, Temperature sensor, Furnace activator, and Air conditioner activator.

Port input events	Port output events
p1. Touch Mode button	p8. Display ambient temperature
p2. Touch Up button	p9. Display desired temperature
p3. Touch Down button	p10. Turn furnace On
p4. Sense ambient temperature	p11. Turn furnace Off
p5. Display timeout	p12. Turn air conditioner On
p6. Non-furnace heat	p13. Turn air conditioner Off
p7. Non-AC cooling	

Data places

d1. Off	d7. Furnace Off
d2. Heating mode active	d8. Air conditioner On
d3. Cooling mode active	d9. Air conditioner Off
d4. Ambient temperature	d10. Too warm
d5. Desired temperature	d11. Too cool
d6. Furnace On	d12. Temp OK

3.3.5 Railroad Crossing Gate Controller

In a town in northern Illinois, there is a railroad crossing where Poplar Avenue crosses the Chicago North Western railroad tracks. There are three separate tracks at the intersection, and each track has sensors to detect when a train approaches the intersection and when it leaves. When no trains are present (or approaching), the crossing gate is up. When the first train approaches, the crossing gate is lowered, and when the last train leaves, the gate is raised. If a second or third train arrives while a train is in the intersection, there is no action on the gate (because it is already down).

Port input events
    p1. Train arrival
    p2. Train departure

Port output events
    p3. Lower crossing gate
    p4. Raise crossing gate

Data places
    d1. Number of trains in crossing

3.3.6 The Pizza Robot

The Pizza Robot automates the ordering, assembling, baking, delivery, and reporting aspects of a pizza place. A human attendant is present only for minimal functions, such as replenishing the ingredient supply devices, for identifying the customer, and handing the boxed pizza to the customer. We will assume that a customer can only order one pizza per transaction.

Orders can be placed by telephone or by a walk-up customer interface, similar to the one in the diagram in Figure 3.2. Once the Process Order button is touched, the cost of the pizza is computed and credit card company is contacted. If the amount is approved, the card is directly billed; otherwise the customer is informed that the order cannot be processed.

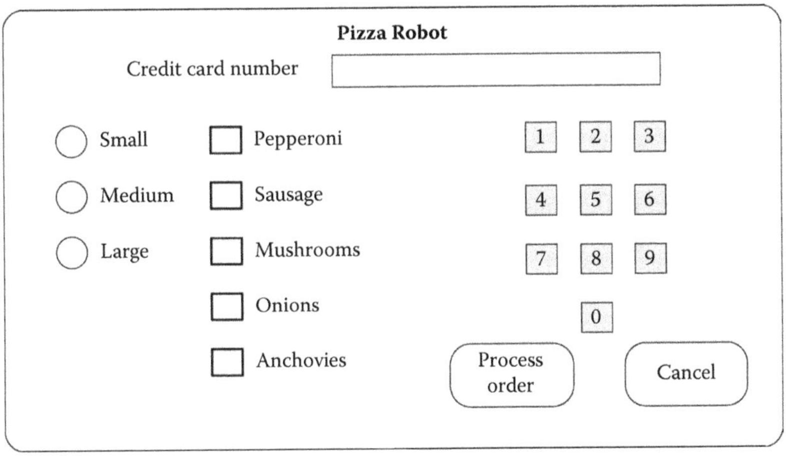

Figure 3.2   Pizza Robot graphical user interface.

Telephone orders use a voice-menu system that obtains the same information as the GUI, with a dialog similar to this:

Size request: Please select the size pizza you wish the Pizza Robot to bake: touch 1 for a small pizza, 2 for a medium pizza, or 3 for a large pizza. Enter a 0 to hear this request again.

Topping request: Every Pizza Robot pizza begins with cheese and special Pizza Robot sauce. You may have any of five topping choices. After each prompt, enter a 1 if you want the item, enter a 2 if you do not want the item.

Do you want pepperoni on your Pizza Robot pizza? Enter 1 for yes, 2 for no.
Do you want sausage on your Pizza Robot pizza? Enter 1 for yes, 2 for no.
Do you want mushrooms on your Pizza Robot pizza? Enter 1 for yes, 2 for no.
Do you want onions on your Pizza Robot pizza? Enter 1 for yes, 2 for no.
Do you want anchovies on your Pizza Robot pizza? Enter 1 for yes, 2 for no.

Order confirmation: If your order is correct, please enter 1. If you wish to repeat your order, please hang up and call again. The cost of your Pizza Robot pizza will appear on your next telephone bill.

Price computation: The price of a Pizza Robot pizza is computed as follows. Small pizza: $8.00, Medium: $10.00, and Large: $12.00. Each topping is 10% of the base pizza price. Thus a small, plain cheese pizza would cost $8.00, and a large pizza with everything would cost $18.00.

Pizza assembly: Once a pizza order is confirmed, the Pizza Robot assembles the pizza with the correct toppings, it computes the proper cooking time, and places it in the oven. Cooking time is a function of pizza size and the number of toppings. This information is preset at the Pizza Robot factory, and is regarded as proprietary information. Cooked pizzas are boxed by the Pizza Robot, and a transaction number is printed on a label and placed on the box.

Pizza delivery: The attendant matches the label with the customer. "No show" customers are out of luck; their phone or credit card is billed anyway, and the attendant usually gives the pizza to a friend. The Pizza Robot constantly monitors the pizza supplies. When any item gets below 10% of normal operating supply, the attendant is prompted to replenish the item.

End-of-day reports: At the end of each business day, the Pizza Robot produces a report showing exactly which pizzas were ordered, the amount of ingredients used, and the totals of the credit card and telephone charges. Telephone charges are sent at the end of the business day to the local phone company.

3.4 Issues in the Examples

Table 3.6 summarizes the behavioral issues present in our set of continuing examples. Two issues are absent from the examples: priority and deadlock. These will be discussed in the appropriate chapters, but they are not present in any of our examples.

Table 3.6   Behavioral Issues in Examples

Issue	1040EZ Tax	NextDate	Espresso Vending	Fuel Pump	Windshield Wiper
Sequence	x	x	x	x	x
Selection	x	x	x	x	x
Repetition	...	...	...	x	x
Enable	...	...	...	x	x
Disable	...	...	x	x	x
Trigger	...	...	...	x	...
Activate	...	...	...	x	...
Suspend	...	...	...	x	...
Resume	...	...	...	x	...
Pause	...	...	...	x	...
Priority	...	...	...	...	...
Mutual exclusion	...	...	...	x	...
Concurrent execution	...	...	...	x	...
Deadlock	...	...	...	...	...
Context-sensitive input events	...	...	x	...	x
Multiple-context output events	...	...	x	x	...
Asynchronous events	...	...	x	x	x
Event quiescence	...	...	x	x	x

References

Bohm, C., and G. Jacopini. 1966. Flow diagrams, Turing machines, and languages with only two formation rules. *Communications of the ACM* 9 (5): 266.

Coleman, D., P. Arnold, S. Bodoff, C. Dollin, and H. Gilchrist. 1994. *Object-oriented development: The fusion method.* Englewood Cliffs, N.J.: Prentice Hall.

Harel, D. and M. Politi. 1998. *Modeling reactive systems with statecharts: the STATEMATE approach.* New York: McGraw-Hill.

Hatley, Derek J. and I. A. Pirbhai. 1988. *Strategies for Real-Time System Specification.* New York: Dorset House Publishing.

Ward, Paul T. and Stephen J. Mellor. 1986. *Structured Development for Real-Time Systems.* Upper Saddle River, NJ: Prentice-Hall.

Exercises

1. Map the five Continuing Examples onto the bar graphs you made for Exercise 1 in Chapter 1.
2. Map the five Reader Examples onto the bar graphs you made for Exercise 1 in Chapter 1.
3. Make issue tables (e.g., Table 3.5) for each of the reader problems.

Chapter 4

Flowcharts

Flowcharts have been in use since the early days of computing; as such, they are likely the earliest behavioral model. In the 1960s, vendors often gave away plastic flowchart templates so that programmers could produce neater diagrams. The IBM Corp. even had a standard flowchart template, with varying sizes of the basic symbols. Some old-timers joke that this was the first CASE (computer-aided software engineering) tool.

4.1 Definition and Notation

There are two distinct styles of flowchart notation. The first, shown in Figure 4.1, is minimalist in the sense that it only has symbols for actions, decisions, and two kinds of page connectors. The off-page connector is used for large systems that cannot fit neatly on a single page. The convention for off-page connectors is to use capital letters, A, B, C..., where the first off-page connection would be A, and the point to which the connection is made (on a separate page) is also labeled with an A.

In the early days of flowchart usage, much attention was paid to Input/Output devices, and this attention was reflected in an expanded set of flowchart symbols similar to the ones shown in Figure 4.2. (There was even a shape for magnetic tape!)

The "flow" portion of the flowchart notation is shown with arrows emanating from and terminating on separate flowchart symbols. Figure 4.3 is a sample flowchart of our Espresso Vending Machine. It will be used to support further discussion of the flowchart technique.

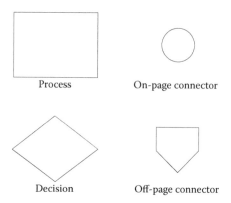

Figure 4.1   Minimalist flowchart symbols.

4.2 Technique

If you look carefully at the flowchart in Figure 4.3, you might notice that arrows generally terminate on the top part of a symbol. This is not mandatory, but it does help comprehension. Decision boxes have exactly one entry point and, because a decision is being made, at least two exit arrows. In the old FORTRAN days, when the language had an "Arithmetic IF" with three outcomes, the sides and bottom vertex of the diamond were used for the three choices (<, =, >). Three decision alternatives are easily shown, as with the Euro coins in Figure 4.3. If more than three alternatives are needed, as in a Case/Switch statement, just use one connecting arrow for each alternative. (Notation is the slave, not the master!) Process boxes, on the other hand, have a maximum of one exit arrow, but they may have several incoming flow arrows.

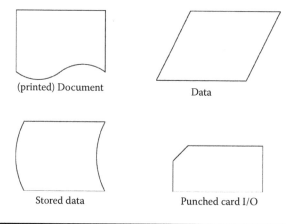

Figure 4.2   I/O device flowchart symbols.

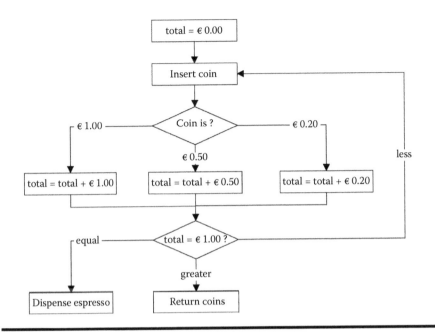

Figure 4.3 Flowchart of the espresso vending machine.

Labels on flow arrows normally refer to the possible outcomes of a decision box: Yes/No, True/False, or values on which the decision is made. Flow arrows emanating from process boxes are not labeled. The intent is that the activity described in the process box is complete, and flow goes to the "next" box. There is no representation of information content flow among boxes. We are asked to imagine that the results of one processing box are "available" to subsequent boxes.

There is very little restriction on the textual content of process and decision boxes. There are distinct styles, and these correspond to levels of abstraction. Box text can be quite general, as in Figure 4.3, or it could be quite specific, almost at the programming language construct level. For example, the "Coin is" decision box has alternatives €1.00, €0.50, and €0.20. Alternatively, the decision condition could be expressed with binary conditions for each coin type, with emanating choices "Yes" and "No." Whichever choice is made, it is good practice to remain consistent; mixing levels of abstraction is undesirable.

The symbol set for flowcharts explicitly supports the three basic constructs of Structured Programming: sequence, selection, and repetition. The decision boxes in Figure 4.3 are all examples of selection. There is one example of repetition: Near the bottom of Figure 4.3, the "less" alternative of the comparison of total with €1.00 flows back to the insert coin process box. The €1.00 branch, which terminates with the "dispense espresso" process box, is an example of sequence. The Single Entry, Single Exit convention of Structured Programming is not necessarily enforced, but it is in Figure 4.3.

The flowchart notation can deal with levels of abstraction by using a form of hierarchy. A high-level process box, for example, can be expanded in more detail in a separate flowchart. If this is done, either the lower level flowchart should be named so that is clearly a decomposition of the higher level process box, or off-page connectors can be used. (The latter choice is more cumbersome.) Table 4.1, summarizes the control issues that can be represented in flowcharts.

Table 4.1 Representation of Behavioral Issues with Flowcharts

Issue	Represented?	Comment
Sequence	yes	Main point of flowcharts
Selection	yes	Main point of flowcharts
Repetition	yes	Main point of flowcharts
Enable	no	Must describe as text in a process box
Disable	no	Must describe as text in a process box
Trigger	no	Must describe as text in a process box
Activate	no	Must describe as text in a process box
Suspend	no	Must describe as text in a process box
Resume	no	Must describe as text in a process box
Pause	no	Must describe as text in a process box
Conflict	no	…
Priority	no	Must describe as text in a process box
Mutual exclusion	no	Parallel paths after a decision
Concurrent execution	no	Must describe as text in a process box
Deadlock	no	…
Context-sensitive input events	no	Must be deduced by careful examination of sequences following a decision
Multiple-context output events	indirectly	Must be deduced by careful examination of sequences following a decision
Asynchronous events	no	…
Event quiescence	no	…

4.3 Continuing Examples

The variable names and other notations used in these figures are taken from those defined in Chapter 3. Usually, a process box is used to indicate that variables have (or are getting) values. Also, process boxes may be used to show that events occur.

4.3.1 Simplified U.S. 1040EZ Income Tax Form

The flowchart in Figure 4.4 exactly describes the calculation steps and decisions needed to compute one's income tax using form U.S. 1040EZ. Notice that all inputs are obtained in the first process box, making this a good example of a transformational (rather than a reactive) system. Also notice that all variables receive values before they are used. There is a minor predisposition here: The AGI (adjusted gross income) quantity is computed before the minStDed, but they could be computed in the reverse order.

The flowchart representation of U.S. 1040EZ works very well. The sequential information, the calculations, and the necessary decisions are all shown. There

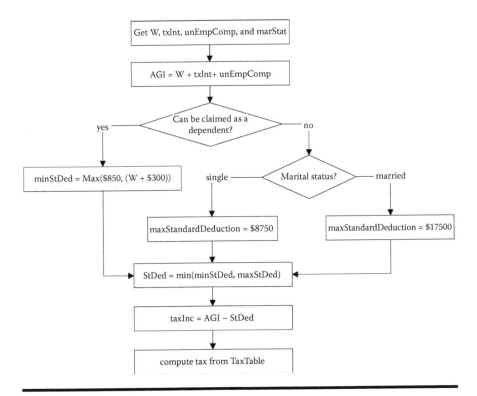

Figure 4.4   U.S. 1040EZ form (from 2007).

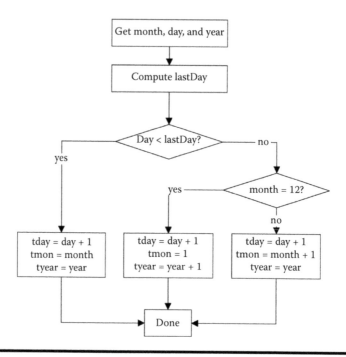

Figure 4.5 NextDate function.

are no event-based issues, nor are there any ESML (Extended Systems Modeling Language) prompt issues. Although no repetition is needed for this example, flowcharts show looping easily.

4.3.2 The NextDate Function

Figures 4.5 and 4.6 show how flowcharts represent hierarchy and functional decomposition. The value of the variable lastDay is computed "offline" and then used in

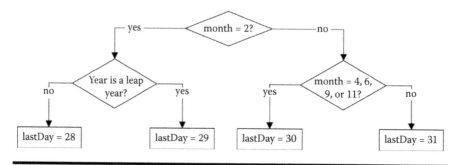

Figure 4.6 Details of lastDay calculation.

the comparison with "day" in the decision box. When a variable gets a value at more than one place, we must ensure that the computed values don't overwrite each other when the flow lines are followed. In the NextDate flowchart, there are three assignments of values to tmon. The decision boxes force these three assignments to be mutually exclusive. (Incidentally, these calculations show the apparent use of GoTo statements, a common practice when flowcharts were the dominant behavioral model.)

The NextDate function is logic-intensive, and this is displayed well in the flowchart. Similarly, the sequential information is also shown well, but as with U.S. 1040EZ, there is no looping. Also, there are no issues of ESML prompts or task-interaction constructs. Finally, there are no events in NextDate.

4.3.3 Espresso Vending Machine

See Figure 4.3 in Section 4.2. The flowchart in Figure 4.3 captures some of the Espresso Vending Machine problem, but it misses much more, as we will see in the finite state machine model (Chapter 6). Events are named and shown in process boxes. We could use a special input or output symbol for the events, but this really adds very little. One problem is that the "insert coin" event is very general. The type of coin is determined in the next decision box, so the appropriate calculations are indicated. The various coin-insertion sequences, both sensible and unexpected, are not shown, making it difficult to develop test cases that exercise these sequences. Also, the coin-return event, which can occur at any time in a transaction, is not shown.

4.3.4 Smart Fuel Pump

Some of the limitations of flowcharts are seen in Figure 4.7. Selection of fuel grade and payment mode can occur in either order, but the flowchart forces the payment mode to be chosen first. The Smart Fuel Pump is an event-driven (reactive) system, so it will be difficult to express the variety of possible event sequences with a flowchart. Some event sequences are correctly shown; for example, the nozzle must be removed from the holster before the trigger can be squeezed. The issue that arises when the tank level is below 4% is shown only partially. That decision suggests that, if the tank level falls below 4% while gas is being pumped, the transaction is ended. The flowchart does not show that this event can occur at any time during a fueling transaction. Note that the "more gas?" decision is made by the customer, not the system. Also, note that time is explicitly not represented. For how long does the "squeeze trigger" last? We understand it to be determined by the person holding the nozzle/trigger. The best we can do here is to add a "more gas?" decision.

There are some ESML prompting behaviors in the Smart Fuel Pump, but these are not shown in the flowchart. For example, the approval, either by the attendant

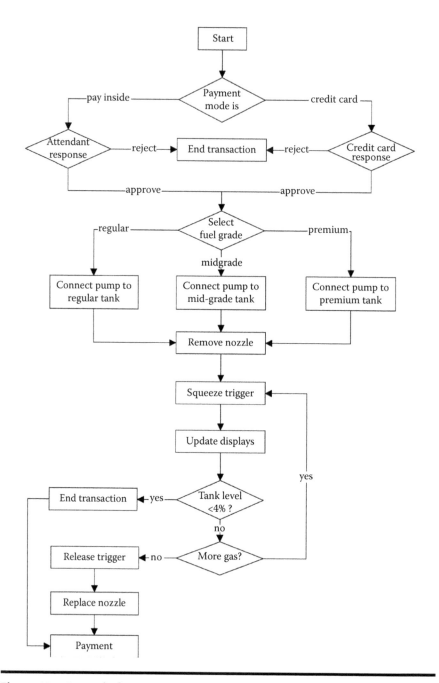

Figure 4.7 Smart fuel pump.

or by the credit card company, would be perfectly represented by the ESML Enable prompt. Also, the 4% fuel level event, which can occur at any time, would be well represented as an ESML Suspend. The trigger squeeze and release events actually interact with two processes, fuel delivery and display updating. Both would be well represented by the ESML Activate prompt, which is also the sequence of ESML Enable followed by ESML Disable.

Finally, there are several points that should be identified as event quiescent, but these are not represented in the flowchart. One example is the trigger release event: The fuel pump must wait until some event occurs, but this is not shown. In general, flowcharts can show event quiescence by having polling or waiting loops, but this easily becomes cumbersome.

4.3.5 *Saturn Windshield Wiper Controller*

The Saturn Windshield Wiper is a purely event-driven system. It is nicely represented as a finite state machine, and even better, as a statechart. In the flowchart, we see two uses of decision boxes: The first ("lever at Int?") asks about the state of the lever, and the second type is where the type of event ("event is?") is determined by decision-box outcomes. The looping shown in Figure 4.8 is close to the reality of the windshield wiper, but it is subtly embedded in the nested decision-based loops. It would be difficult to develop test cases from the flowchart representation.

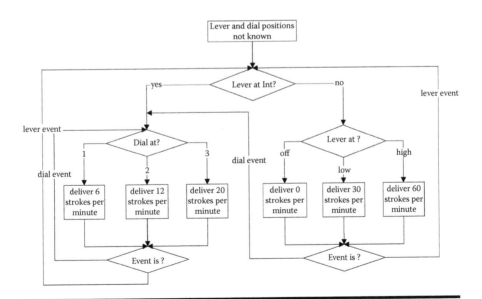

Figure 4.8   Saturn windshield wiper controller.

4.4 Selected Examples for Readers

Two examples are started here, mostly to give a flavor of what the elusive "conscientious reader" might do.

4.4.1 Saturn Cruise Control

Figure 4.9 shows only a simple part of the Saturn cruise control system—the normal case in which the driver brings the car to a desired speed, turns on the cruise control system, and sets the desired speed. The feedback loop is intended to show the response of the system to external influences on the car, such as hills. The feedback loop is meant to be continuous, but there is no flowchart mechanism to show this.

Flowcharts break down here, due to the extremely event-driven nature of the Saturn Cruise Control system. We would need decision boxes for the following driver input events, which could occur in any order and at any point in the flowchart:

- Touch Cruise On/Off
- Touch Set/Coast
- Hold Set/Coast for less than 0.5 seconds

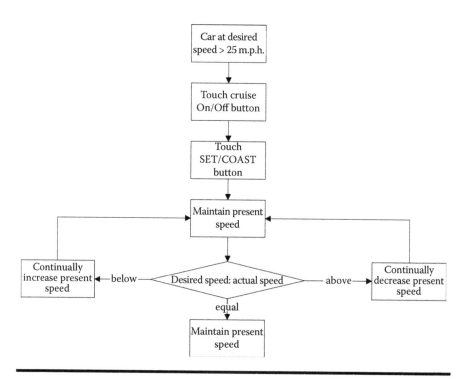

Figure 4.9 Partial Saturn cruise control.

- Hold Set/Coast for more than 0.5 seconds
- Touch Res/AcceL
- Hold Res/AcceL for less than 0.5 seconds
- Hold Res/AcceL for more than 0.5 seconds
- Touch brake pedal
- Driver accelerate to desired speed
- Driver decelerate to desired speed
- Driver release accelerator pedal

4.4.2 The Pizza Robot

The Pizza Robot flowchart in Figure 4.10 contains another example of the use of hierarchy to simplify a logically complex problem. The sequential decision making

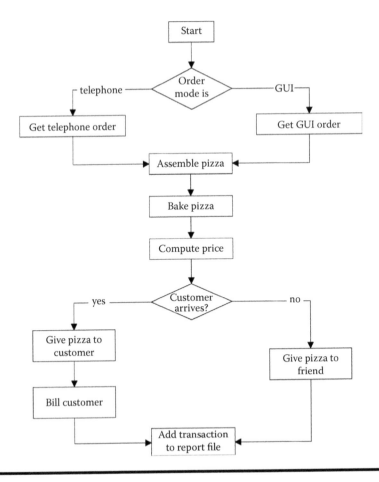

Figure 4.10   Pizza robot.

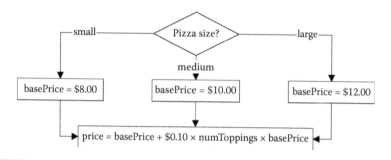

Figure 4.11   Compute price flowchart.

forced by the telephone order process is condensed into one process box at the high level. The compression of the event-driven GUI (graphical user interface) order process is even more dramatic. Each of these would be expanded into lower level flowcharts. Figure 4.11 contains the expansion of the price computation process; it assumes that the order processes compute the number of requested toppings and obtain the pizza size. The process box in which the final price is computed is a good example of how a flowchart can be almost like source code. Notice the implicit assumption that variables obtain values "earlier" in a flowchart.

4.5 Advantages and Limitations

Flowcharts have several clear advantages. Any notation that has been used for 50 years must have something going for it. In the case of flowcharts, it is ease of comprehension. Since text in process and decision boxes can be natural language, flowcharts improve understanding between customers and developers. (Even the U.S. Internal Revenue Service uses flowcharts to explain complicated parts of the tax code.) As noted earlier, flowcharts express the basic structured programming constructs. This means that any "well-formed" flowchart can be coded in an imperative, structured programming language. As we have seen in our examples, flowcharts support levels of abstraction; therefore they can scale up to describe large, complex applications. Another advantage is that they can be used to describe complex computations and algorithms. Finally, some control (or behavior) is represented by the different paths through a flowchart.

There are limitations to flowcharts. The very nature of sequence makes it extremely difficult to describe event-driven systems in which independent events can occur in any order. In Figure 4.7, for example, the sequence forces the payment mode choice before the fuel grade selection can be made; the requirements explicitly state that these can be done in either order. Secondly, there is no simple way to describe the context of external devices in which the system being described operates. (The device-oriented I/O symbols might work for this purpose, but there would be many extensions.) There is very little representation of data. The text in process and decision boxes can contain variable names, but this is very rudimentary. Since data representation is scant, there is even less opportunity to express data structure and relationships among data. There is also potential confusion about process boxes and "where" they are executed. Note in Figure 4.7 that several process boxes actually refer to external events (e.g., the squeeze- and release-trigger boxes).

Exercises

1. Find examples of flowcharts in noncomputing situations. Discuss how effectively they communicate the problem being discussed.
2. Express the Windchill Factor Table problem as a flowchart. Discuss how well the problem is represented.
3. Express the Previous Date problem as a flowchart. Discuss how well the problem is represented.
4. Express the Saturn Cruise Control problem as a flowchart. Discuss how well the problem is represented.
5. Express the Programmable Thermostat problem as a flowchart. Discuss how well the problem is represented.
6. Express the Railroad Crossing Gate Controller problem as a flowchart. Discuss how well the problem is represented.
7. Express the Six-Coin Espresso Vending Machine problem (see Chapter 3) as a flowchart. Compare your flowchart to the one in the text. Does the simplification make the flowchart model any more useful?
8. Derek Coleman's original version of the "petrol pump" includes the possibility of a New Zealand pump, which permits a customer to define either a maximum volume or a maximum price for a transaction. Modify the fuel pump flowchart to show this extension.

Chapter 5

Decision Tables

Decision tables have been used to represent and analyze complex logical relationships for decades. They are ideal for describing situations in which a number of combinations of actions are taken under varying sets of conditions. Some of the basic decision table terms are illustrated in Table 5.1

5.1 Definition and Notation

A decision table has four portions: the part to the left of the bold vertical line is the stub portion; to the right is the entry portion. The part above the bold horizontal line is the condition portion, and below is the action portion. Thus, we can refer to the condition stub, the condition entries, the action stub, and the action entries. A column in the entry portion is a rule. Rules indicate which actions, if any, are taken for the circumstances indicated in the condition portion of the rule. In the decision table in Table 5.1, when conditions c_1, c_2, and c_3 are all true, actions a_1 and a_2 occur (rule 1). When c_1 and c_2 are both true and c_3 is false, actions a_1 and a_3 occur (rule 2).

When we have binary conditions (true/false, yes/no, 0/1), the condition portion of a decision table is a truth table (from propositional logic) that has been rotated 90°. This structure guarantees that we consider every possible combination of condition values. Decision tables are deliberately declarative (as opposed to imperative); no particular order is implied by the conditions; selected actions do not occur in any particular order; and rules can be written in any order. This latitude is sometimes handy to express normal cases as the first few rules, and exceptional cases later.

Table 5.1 Parts of a Decision Table

Stub	Rule 1	Rule 2	Rule 3	Rule 4	Rule 5	Rule 6	Rule 7	Rule 8
c1	T	T	T	T	F	F	F	F
c2	T	T	F	F	T	T	F	F
c3	T	F	T	F	T	F	T	F
a1	x	x	...	...	x	...	...	...
a2	x	...	...	...	...	...	...	...
a3	...	x	...	...	...	x	x	x
a4	...	...	x	x	x	...	x	x

Definition

Decision tables in which all of the conditions are binary are called *limited-entry decision tables*. A limited-entry decision table with n conditions has 2^n distinct rules.

Definition

Decision tables in which all of the conditions have a finite number of alternative values are called *extended-entry decision tables*.

Definition

Decision tables in which some conditions have a finite number of alternative values and others are strictly binary are called *mixed-entry decision tables*.

Decision tables presume that all the values necessary to evaluate conditions are available at the onset of table rule execution. Decision table actions may be used to change the values of variables, and this may occur in conjunction with a "repeat table" action. There is also a notion of hierarchy: Actions may invoke other decision tables.

5.2 Decision Table Analysis

The rigorous structure of decision tables supports some interesting algebraic manipulations.

5.2.1 Decision Table Condensation

When two (or more) rules have identical action entries, there must be a condition that is true in one rule and false in another. Clearly, then, that condition has no

Table 5.2   Logically Condensed Version of Table 5.1

Stub	Rule 1	Rule 2	Rules 3, 4	Rule 5	Rule 6	Rules 7, 8
c1	T	T	T	F	F	F
c2	T	T	F	T	T	F
c3	T	F	—	T	F	—
a1	X	X	...	X	...	...
a2	X	...	...	...	...	...
a3	...	X	...	...	X	X
a4	...	...	X	X	...	X

effect on the actions that are performed in those rules. Table 5.2 shows the result of this logical condensation on the decision table in Table 5.1.

Definition

If a condition has no effect on the actions performed by two rules, the rule entry for that condition is a *Don't Care* entry, usually written as a long dash (—).

The entry for c3 in the rule where c1 is true and c2 is false is a Don't Care entry. The Don't Care entry has two major interpretations: The condition is irrelevant, or the condition does not apply. Sometimes people will enter the "n/a" symbol for this latter interpretation.

5.2.2 Decision Tables with Mutually Exclusive Conditions

When conditions refer to equivalence classes, decision tables have a characteristic appearance. Conditions in the decision table in Table 5.3 are from the NextDate

Table 5.3   Decision Table with Mutually Exclusive Rules

Conditions	Rule 1	Rule 2	Rule 3
c1. 30-day month?	T	—	—
c2. 31-day month?	—	T	—
c3. February?	—	—	T
a1			
a2			
a3			

Table 5.4 Decision Table for Table 5.3 with Rule Counts

Conditions	Rule 1	Rule 2	Rule 3
c1. 30-day month?	T	—	—
c2. 31-day month?	—	T	—
c3. February?	—	—	T
a1			
Rule count	4	4	4

problem; they refer to the mutually exclusive possibilities for the month variable. Because a month is in exactly one equivalence class, we cannot ever have a rule in which two entries are true. The Don't Care entries (—) really mean "must be false." Some decision table aficionados use the notation F! to make this point.

Use of Don't Care entries has a subtle effect on the way in which complete decision tables are recognized. For limited-entry decision tables, if n conditions exist, there must be 2^n distinct rules. When Don't Care entries really indicate that the condition is irrelevant, we can develop a rule count as follows: Rules in which no Don't Care entries occur count as one rule, and each Don't Care entry in a rule doubles the count of that rule. The rule counts for the decision table in Table 5.3 are shown below in Table 5.4. Notice that the sum of the rule counts is 12 (as it should be).

If we applied this simplistic algorithm to the decision table in Table 5.4, we get the rule counts shown in Table 5.5.

Table 5.5 Expanded Decision Table for Table 5.3 with Rule Counts

Conditions	Rule 1	Rule 2	Rule 3	Rule 4	Rule 5	Rule 6	Rule 7	Rule 8	Rule 9	Rule 10	Rule 11	Rule 12
c1. 30-day?	T	T	T	T	T	T	F	F	T	T	F	F
c2. 31-day?	T	T	F	F	T	T	T	T	T	F	T	F
c3. February?	T	F	T	F	T	F	T	F	T	T	T	T
a1												
Rule count	1	1	1	1	1	1	1	1	1	1	1	1

Table 5.6   Expanded Decision Table for Table 5.3 with Impossible Rules

Conditions	Rule 1	Rule 2	Rule 3	Rule 4	Rule 5	Rule 6	Rule 7	Rule 8	Rule 9	Rule 10	Rule 11	Rule 12
c1. 30-day?	T	T	T	T	T	T	F	F	T	T	F	F
c2. 31-day?	T	T	F	F	T	T	T	T	T	F	T	F
c3. February?	T	F	T	F	T	F	T	F	T	T	T	T
a1												
Impossible?	Y	Y	Y	N	Y	Y	Y	N	Y	Y	Y	N

We should only have eight rules, so we clearly have a problem. To see where the problem lies, we expand each of the three rules, replacing the "—" entries with the T and F possibilities, as shown in Table 5.5.

Notice that we have three rules in which all entries are T: rules 1, 5, and 9. We also have two rules with T, T, F entries: rules 2 and 6. Similarly, rules 3 and 10 are identical; so are rules 7 and 11. If we delete the repetitions, we end up with seven rules; the missing rule is the one in which all conditions are false. The result of this process in shown in Table 5.6. The impossible rules are also shown. If we eliminate the impossible rules, and use the "F!" (must be false) notation to emphasize the mutual exclusion, we arrive at Table 5.7, which is a more accurate way to show the mutual exclusion in Table 5.3.

5.2.3 Redundant and Inconsistent Decision Tables

The ability to recognize (and develop) complete decision tables puts us in a powerful position with respect to redundancy and inconsistency. The decision table in

Table 5.7   Elimination of Impossible Rules

Conditions	Rule 4	Rule 8	Rule 12
c1. 30-day?	T	F!	F!
c2. 31-day?	F!	T	F!
c3. February?	F!	F!	T
a1			
Impossible?	N	N	N

Table 5.8   A Redundant Decision Table

Stub	Rules 1–4	Rule 5	Rule 6	Rule 7	Rule 8	Rule 9
c1	T	F	F	F	F	T
c2	–	T	T	F	F	F
c3	–	T	F	T	F	F
a1	X	X	X	–	–	X
a2	–	X	X	X	–	–
a3	X	–	X	X	X	X

Table 5.8 is redundant — three conditions and nine rules exist. (Rule 9 is identical to rules 1–4.)

Notice that the action entries in rule 9 are identical to those in rules 1–4. As long as the actions in a redundant rule are identical to the corresponding part of the decision table, we do not have much of a problem. If the action entries are different, as they are in Table 5.9, we have a bigger problem.

If the decision table in Table 5.9 were to process a transaction in which c1 is true and both c2 and c3 are false, both rules 4 and 9 apply. We can make two observations:

1. Rules 4 and 9 are inconsistent.
2. The decision table is nondeterministic.

Rules 4 and 9 are inconsistent because the action sets are different. The whole table is nondeterministic because there is no way to decide whether to apply rule 4 or rule 9.

Table 5.9   An Inconsistent Decision Table

Stub	Rules 1–4	Rule 5	Rule 6	Rule 7	Rule 8	Rule 9
c1	T	F	F	F	F	T
c2	–	T	T	F	F	F
c3	–	T	F	T	F	F
a1	X	X	X	–	–	–
a2	–	X	X	X	–	X
a3	X	–	X	X	X	–

Table 5.10   U.S. 1040EZ Decision Table (Part 1)

Conditions	Rule 1	Rule 2	Rule 3	Rule 4
c1. Can be claimed as a dependent?	Yes	Yes	No	No
c2. Marital status is	–	–	married	single
a1. Compute minStandardDeduction	X	X	...	...
a2. maxStandardDeduction = $8750	...	...	...	X
a3 maxStandardDeduction = $17500	...	...	X	...
a4. Compute Standard Deduction	X	X	X	X
a5. Compute taxable income	X	X	X	X
a6. Compute tax from Tax Table	X	X	X	X

5.3 Continuing Examples

5.3.1 Simplified U.S. 1040EZ Income Tax Form

There is not much decision making in the Simplified U.S. 1040EZ Income Tax Form; therefore its decision table representation is not a particularly good choice (Table 5.10). As noted earlier, we can assume that the input variables have values that are used in the actions to produce output variables.

Since c2 is a Don't Care condition, we can combine rules 1 and 2, leaving a decision table (Table 5.11) that exactly echoes the decision-making part of the flowchart in Figure 4.4.

Table 5.11   U.S. 1040EZ Decision Table (Part 2)

Conditions	Rules 1, 2	Rule 3	Rule 4
c1. Can be claimed as a dependent?	Yes	No	No
c2. Marital status is	–	married	single
a1. Compute minStandardDeduction	X	...	...
a2. maxStandardDeduction = $8,750	...	...	X
a3. maxStandardDeduction = $17,500	...	X	...
a4. Compute Standard Deduction	X	X	X
a5. Compute taxable income	X	X	X
a6. Compute tax from Tax Table	X	X	X

No sequential steps of the U.S. 1040EZ problem are shown in the decision table description. Also, there is a necessary order to the actions, but this order cannot be enforced, due to the declarative nature of decision tables. One work-around might be to use numbers instead of X entries to show the order in which actions should be executed.

5.3.2 The NextDate Function

The NextDate function was chosen for its decisional complexity. Here we will see that identifying the right conditions is a critical step in developing a decision table. We will use conditions based on equivalence classes of the three variables: month, day, and year. As with many modeling techniques, there is no reason to believe that a first attempt is perfect; iteration is always a good idea when developing any kind of model.

5.3.2.1 First Try

The equivalence classes used here are also found in *Software Testing: A Craftsman's Approach* (Jorgensen 2008), where the NextDate example is used because it is the basis of decision table–based testing. Because equivalence classes are disjoint, they are perfect for conditions in an extended-entry decision table.

$M1 = \{\text{month : month has 30 days}\}$
$M2 = \{\text{month : month has 31 days}\}$
$M3 = \{\text{month : month is February}\}$
$D1 = \{\text{day : } 1 \leq \text{day} \leq 28\}$
$D2 = \{\text{day : day} = 29\}$
$D3 = \{\text{day : day} = 30\}$
$D4 = \{\text{day : day} = 31\}$
$Y1 = \{\text{year : year is a leap year}\}$
$Y2 = \{\text{year : year is not a leap year}\}$

These nine equivalence classes translate into eight conditions (the False entry for c8 gives us Y2):

c1. month in M1 c5. day in D2
c2. month in M2 c6. day in D3
c3. month in M3 c7. day in D4
c4. day in D1 c8. year in Y1

Regardless of the conditions, we will have these actions:

a1. impossible a4. increment month
a2. increment day a5. reset month
a3. reset day a6. increment year

Table 5.12 NextDate Subtable

Conditions	
c2. month in M2?	Yes
c7. day in D4?	–
a3. reset day	X
a4. increment month	?
a5. reset month	?
a6. increment year	?

If we use these eight conditions to form a limited-entry decision table, we will have 256 rules—far too many to be useful. This brings to mind an old quotation from Richard Hamming (1962): "The purpose of computing is insight, not numbers." We can substitute modeling for computing, and conclude that this extreme size is undesirable. Take a closer look at the subtable in Table 5.12, where we look at the last day of a 31-day month. If the month is December, we perform actions a3 and a4; if it is any other 31-day month, we only perform actions a1 and a2. This problem exists because of logical dependencies among the month, day, and year variables. Clearly, month = December requires special treatment, so we revise our equivalence classes.

5.3.2.2 Second Try

With this improved set of equivalence classes, we shift to an extended-entry decision table. For space reasons, we break it into subtables (Tables 5.13, 5.14, and 5.15).

M1 = {month : month has 30 days}
M2 = {month : month has 31 days, but not December}
M3 = {month : month is December}
M4 = {month : month is February}
D1 = {day : 1 ≤ day ≤ 28}
D2 = {day : day = 29}
D3 = {day : day = 30}
D4 = {day : day = 31}
Y1 = {year : year is a leap year}
Y2 = {year : year is not a leap year}

There is another equivalence class problem for February, since the last day can be either 28 or 29 (Table 5.16).

Table 5.13   30-Day Month Subtable

Conditions				
c1. month in ?	M1	M1	M1	M1
c2. day in ?	D1	D2	D3	D4
a1. impossible	—	—	—	X
a2. increment day	X	X	—	—
a3. reset day	—	—	X	—
a4. increment month	—	—	X	—
a5. reset month	—	—	—	—
a6. increment year	—	—	—	—

5.3.2.3 Third Try

We can clear up the end-of-year considerations with a third set of equivalence classes. This time, we are very specific about days and months.

$M1 = \{month : month\ has\ 30\ days\}$
$M2 = \{month : month\ has\ 31\ days\ except\ December\}$
$M3 = \{month : month\ is\ December\}$
$M4 = \{month : month\ is\ February\}$
$D1 = \{day : 1 \leq day \leq 27\}$
$D2 = \{day : day = 28\}$

Table 5.14   31-Day Month (Except December) Subtable

Conditions				
c1. month in ?	M2	M2	M2	M2
c2. day in ?	D1	D2	D3	D4
a1. impossible	—	—	—	—
a2. increment day	X	X	X	—
a3. reset day	—	—	—	X
a4. increment month	—	—	—	X
a5. reset month	—	—	—	—
a6. increment year	—	—	—	—

Table 5.15 December Subtable

Conditions				
c1. month in ?	M3	M3	M3	M3
c2. day in ?	D1	D2	D3	D4
a1. impossible	—	—	—	—
a2. increment day	X	X	X	—
a3. reset day	—	—	—	X
a4. increment month	—	—	—	—
a5. reset month	—	—	—	X
a6. increment year	—	—	—	X

$D3 = \{day : day = 29\}$
$D4 = \{day : day = 30\}$
$D5 = \{day : day = 31\}$
$Y1 = \{year : year\ is\ a\ leap\ year\}$
$Y2 = \{year : year\ is\ a\ common\ year\}$

Table 5.16 February Subtable

Conditions										
c1. month in ?	M4	M4	M4	M4	M4	M4	M4	M4	M4	M4
c2. day is ?	<28	28	29	30	31	<28	28	29	30	31
c3. leap year?	N	N	N	N	N	Y	Y	Y	Y	Y
a1. impossible	—	—	X	X	X	—	—	—	X	X
a2. increment day	X	—	—	—	—	X	X	—	—	—
a3. reset day	—	X	—	—	—	—	—	X	—	—
a4. increment month	—	X	—	—	—	—	—	X	—	—
a5. reset month	—	—	—	—	—	—	—	—	—	—
a6. increment year	—	—	—	—	—	—	—	—	—	—

Table 5.17 Full NextDate Decision Table (First Part)

Conditions	1	2	3	4	5	6	7	8	9	10
c1. month in ?	M1	M1	M1	M1	M1	M2	M2	M2	M2	M2
c2. day is ?	D1	D2	D3	D4	D5	D1	D2	D3	D4	D5
c3. leap year?	–	–	–	–	–	–	–	–	–	–
a1. impossible	–	–	X	X	X	–	–	–	X	X
a2. increment day	X	–	–	–	–	X	X	–	–	–
a3. reset day	–	X	–	–	–	–	–	X	–	–
a4. increment month	–	X	–	–	–	–	–	X	–	–
a5. reset month	–	–	–	–	–	–	–	–	–	–
a6. increment year	–	–	–	–	–	–	–	–	–	–

The Cartesian product of these contains 40 elements. The result of combining rules with Don't Care entries is given in Table 5.14; it has 22 rules, compared with the 36 of the second try. Here, we have a 22-rule decision table (Tables 5.17 and 5.18) that gives a clearer picture of the NextDate function than does the 36-rule decision table. The first five rules deal with 30-day months; notice that the leap year considerations are irrelevant. The next two sets of rules (6–15) deal with 31-day months, whereas rules 6–10 deal with months other than December, and rules 11–15 deal with December. No impossible rules are listed in this portion of the decision table, although there is some redundancy that an efficient tester might question. Eight of the ten rules simply increment the day. Finally, the last seven rules focus on February in common and leap years.

We can use the algebra of decision tables to further simplify these 22 test cases. If the action sets of two rules in a limited-entry decision table are identical, there must be at least one condition that allows two rules to be combined with a Don't Care entry. This is the decision table equivalent of the "treated the same" guideline that we used to identify equivalence classes. In a sense, we are identifying equivalence classes of rules. For example, rules 1, 2, and 3 involve day classes D1, D2, and D3 for 30-day months. These can be combined similarly for day classes D1, D2, D3, and D4 in the 31-day month rules, and D4 and D5 for February. The result is shown in Table 5.19.

Table 5.18 Full NextDate Decision Table (Second Part)

Conditions	11	12	13	14	15	16	17	18	19	20	21	22
c1. month in ?	M3	M3	M3	M3	M3	M4	M4	M4	M4	M4	M4	M4
c2. day is ?	D1	D2	D3	D4	D5	D1	D2	D2	D3	D3	D4	D5
c3. leap year?	—	—	—	—	—	—	Y	N	Y	N	—	—
a1. impossible	—	—	—	—	—	—	—	—	—	X	X	X
a2. increment day	X	X	X	X		X	X	—	—	—	—	—
a3. reset day	—	—	—	—	X	—	—	X	X	—	—	—
a4. increment month	—	—	—	—	—	—	—	X	X	—	—	—
a5. reset month	—	—	—	—	X	—	—	—	—	—	—	—
a6. increment year	—	—	—	—	X	—	—	—	—	—	—	—

Table 5.19 Reduced NextDate Decision Table

Conditions	1–3	4	5	6–9	10	11–14	15	16	17	18	19	20	21, 22
c1. month in ?	M1	M1	M1	M2	M2	M3	M3	M4	M4	M4	M4	M4	M4
c2. day is ?	D1, D2, D3	D4	D5	D1, D2, D3, D4	D5	D1, D2, D3, D4	D5	D1	D2	D2	D3	D3	D4, D5
c3. leap year?	—	—	—	—	—	—	—	—	Y	N	Y	N	—
a1. impossible	—	—	X	—	—	—	—	—	—	—	—	X	X
a2. increment day	X	—	—	X		X	X	X	X	—	—	—	—
a3. reset day	—	X	—	—	X	—	X	—	—	X	X	—	—
a4. increment month	—	X	—	—	X	—	—	—	—	X	X	—	—
a5. reset month	—	—	—	—	—	—	X	—	—	—	—	—	—
a6. increment year	—	—	—	—	—	—	X	—	—	—	—	—	—

Decision tables are the ideal model for NextDate, primarily because they elegantly express the dependencies among the equivalence classes of input variables. Lack of order is not even a problem, because, in any given rule, the order in which actions are executed is immaterial.

5.3.3 Espresso Vending Machine

This is an event-driven problem, with four input events and two output events:

Input Events	**Output Events**	**Data**
e1: insert €1 coin	e5: (no action)	d1: coin total
e2: insert €0.20 coin	e6: dispense espresso	
e3: insert €0.50 coin	e7: return coins	
e4: return all coins		

The espresso machine must accept Euro coins, keep track of the total value inserted, and dispense one espresso when (at least) one Euro has been deposited. The possible coin totals, since they are disjoint, are likely candidates for an extended-entry condition with nine entries:

c_1. coin total is: 0.00, 0.20, 0.40, 0.60, 0.80, 0.50, 0.70, 0.90, 1.00

Similarly, the coin inserted can be an extended-entry condition:

c_2. coin is: €0.20 coin, €0.50 coin, €1 coin

The last condition is binary, and refers to whether or not the return all coins event has occurred.

c_3. return all coins

Three of the actions are obvious, but we need three more:

a1. (no action)	a3. return coins	a5. repeat table
a2. dispense espresso	a4. compute total	a6. impossible

Action a1 (no action) is curious. Sometimes this is a handy practice, because otherwise, a blank entry can be ambiguous. In one sense, a blank action entry means do not do that action. A no-action entry makes this explicit. These conditions and actions will give us a mixed-entry decision table with 54 rules, three conditions, and four actions. Even this simple problem shows an inherent problem with decision tables—size that grows exponentially. (I sometimes joke with my graduate classes about Jorgensen's First Law of Software Engineering: Multiplying big numbers by big numbers yields a really big number.) Table 5.20 is a subtable with the first nine rules.

Table 5.20   First Nine Rules of the Espresso Machine Decision Table

Conditions	1	2	3	4	5	6	7	8	9
c1. coin total is ?	0.00	0.20	0.40	0.60	0.80	0.50	0.70	0.90	1.00
c2. coin is ?	0.20	0.20	0.20	0.20	0.20	0.20	0.20	0.20	0.20
c3. return all coins?	N	N	N	N	N	N	N	N	N
a1. (no action)	X	X	X	X	—	X	X	—	X
a2. dispense espresso	—	—	—	—	X	—	—	X	—
a3. return coins	—	—	—	—	—	—	—	—	—
a4. compute total	X	X	X	X	—	X	X	—	—
a5. repeat table	X	X	X	X	—	X	X	—	—
a6. impossible	—	—	—	—	—	—	—	—	X

Look carefully at rule 8: the machine has €0.90 and a €0.20 coin is deposited. What actions should occur? If it is a greedy machine, or if the customer is really desperate for an espresso, the machine dispenses the espresso and keeps the extra €0.10. A customer-friendly choice for this rule is to note that it is impossible, return all coins, and repeat the table. Who makes this decision, the developer or the customer? This is a perfect example of how decision tables can be provocative, in the sense explained in Chapter 1. A responsible developer would recognize this question and know to ask the customer for the preferred choice. This is one place where we see an advantage of decision tables over flowcharts. All of the rules in which this choice occurs are obvious in the full decision table, but they are only suggested by the flowchart (see Figure 4.3).

Now look at rule 9. Why is it impossible? The only ways for the total to be exactly €1.00 is for rules 1–5 to have been executed (in that order), or for two €0.50 coins to have been deposited, or for one €1.00 coin to have been deposited. This also suggests the need for an additional action to reset the coin total after the espresso has been dispensed.

Now we can start to see some of the differences among models. The flowchart in Figure 4.3 is certainly simpler than a decision table with 54 rules, but the simplicity suppresses some of the inherent complexity.

How else might we use decision tables to model the espresso machine? One way is to identify three subtables, depending on which coin is inserted, and compress many of the conditions with these:

    c1a. coin total is: <= 0.90 with c2a. coin is €0.20
    c1b. coin total is: <= 0.60 with c2a. coin is €0.50

Table 5.21 shows the result.

Table 5.21 Compressing the Espresso Machine Decision Table

Conditions	1–4	5
c1. coin total is ?	< 0.80	= 0.80
c2. coin is ?	0.20	0.20
c3. return all coins?	N	N
a1. (no action)	X	–
a2. dispense espresso	–	X
a3. return coins	–	–
a4. compute total	X	–
a5. repeat table	X	–
a6. impossible	–	–

At first, this seems like it will work, but the rules must be totally disjoint, and that will be difficult with the denominations of Euro coins.

The decision table description of the Espresso Vending Machine does not capture the event-driven nature of the problem. Furthermore, the sequences of coin insertion events are suppressed, making test case identification difficult. Also, there is event quiescence in the application, but it cannot be seen in the decision table model.

5.3.4 Smart Fuel Pump

The Smart Fuel Pump is an event-driven system with 11 input events and 7 output events. Since the input events can occur in any order, and since decision tables are declarative (order free), this will be difficult. Here we will break the problem into time-based stages, and illustrate how one decision table can invoke another. We might call these "communicating decision tables" (Tables 5.22, 5.23, and 5.24).

As expected, the event-driven nature of the Smart Fuel Pump is not shown in the decision tables. There are some subtleties. For example, action a3 (perform select fuel grade table) in the payment mode decision table serves to enable the fuel grade selection decision table. Also, condition c1 in the fuel delivery decision table (tank level is <4%) serves to either suspend or disable the remaining actions. This condition should be part of every decision table, because the event can occur at any time, but again, decision tables do not show time order.

Table 5.22   Payment Mode Decision Table

c1. payment mode is	pay inside		credit card	
c2. attendant response is	approve	reject	—	—
c3. Credit card company response is	—	—	approve	reject
a1. reject transaction	—	X	—	X
a2. approve transaction	X	—	X	—
a3. perform select fuel grade table	X	—	X	—

Table 5.23   Fuel Grade Selection Decision Table

c1. fuel grade is	regular	mid-grade	premium
a1. connect to regular tank	X	—	—
a2. connect to mid-grade tank	—	X	—
a3. connect to premium tank	—	—	X
a4. remove nozzle	X	X	X
a5. perform fuel delivery table	X	X	X

Table 5.24   Fuel-Delivery Decision Table

c1. tank level is < 4%?	Yes	No	
c2. more gas?	—	Yes	No
a1. squeeze trigger	—	X	—
a2. release trigger	—	—	X
a3. update displays	X	X	X
a4. repeat table	—	X	X
a5. end transaction	X	—	X
a6. replace nozzle	X	—	X
a7. make payment	X	—	X

Table 5.25   Saturn Windshield Wiper Controller Decision Table

c1. lever at	Off	Intermittent			Low	High
c2. dial at	—	1	2	3	—	—
a1. 0 wpm	X	—	—	—	—	—
a2. 6 wpm	—	X	—	—	—	—
a3. 12 wpm	—	—	X	—	—	—
a4. 20 wpm	—	—	—	X	—	—
a5. 30 wpm	—	—	—	—	X	—
a6. 60 wpm	—	—	—	—	—	X

Note: wpm = wipes per minute.

5.3.5 *Saturn Windshield Wiper Controller*

The problem statement is almost an extended-entry decision table as it stands; the only difference here is individual actions for the wiper speeds (Table 5.25).

Conditions c1 and c2 refer to states of the dial and lever; there is no indication of the lever and dial move events. Thus the context-sensitive input events cannot be observed in this decision table. In a sense, the rules in which the lever is in the Int position serve to enable the dial positions—at least, they give meaning to the dial positions.

5.4 Decision Table Engines

Even though decision tables are deliberately declarative, they have a structure sufficiently rigorous to support a decision table engine. The input to such a decision table execution engine would be all the information needed to complete the condition entries of a rule. The actions in that rule are then the ones that would be executed. One problem: There is no easy way to control the sequence of executed actions. This could be resolved by using integer entries instead of simple Xs to indicate the execution order of actions in a rule. A decision table engine would be interactive, in the sense that the user would provide sets of values for each rule in the decision table.

5.5 Advantages and Limitations

Decision tables are clearly the model of choice for logic-intensive applications. This is particularly true when conditions refer to equivalence classes that have dependencies, as in NextDate. Also, the ability to algebraically simplify decision tables

Table 5.26 Representation of Behavioral Issues with Decision Tables

Issue	Represented?	Comments
Sequence	no	Decision tables are/should be declarative
Selection	yes	The whole point of decision tables!
Repetition	yes	Must use a repeat table action
Enable	indirectly	An enabling condition in conjunction with remaining enabled conditions
Disable	indirectly	An disabling condition in conjunction with remaining enabled conditions
Trigger	no	…
Activate	indirectly	Only in the sense of successive enabling and disabling rules, *but* there is no sense of order, so this is *very* tenuous
Suspend	indirectly	a True suspending condition in combination with the remaining condition entries, either Don't Care or F!
Resume	no	…
Pause	no	…
Conflict	no	…
Priority	no	…
Mutual exclusion	yes	Rules are mutually exclusive
Concurrent execution	no	…
Deadlock	no	…
Context-sensitive input events	yes	Event is one condition; contexts are separate conditions
Multiple-context output events	yes	Same action(s) in different rules
Asynchronous events	no	…
Event quiescence	no	…

results in an elegant approach to minimization. Calculations can only be expressed as actions, but the absence of order is problematic. Finally, input events must be represented as conditions, and output events as actions, but again, the lack of order makes this approach inadequate for event-driven applications. Table 5.26 summarizes the behavioral issue representation of decision tables.

References

Hamming, R. W. 1962. *Rumerical methods for scientists and Engineers*. New York: McGraw-Hill.
Jorgensen, P. C. 2008. *Software testing: A craftsman's approach*. 3rd ed. New York: Taylor and Francis.

Exercises

1. Find examples of decision tables in noncomputing situations. Discuss how effectively they communicate the problem being addressed.
2. Express the Windchill Factor Table problem as a decision table. Discuss how well the problem is represented.
3. Express the Previous Date problem as a decision table. Discuss how well the problem is represented.
4. Express the Saturn Cruise Control problem as a decision table. Discuss how well the problem is represented.
5. Express the Programmable Thermostat problem as a decision table. Discuss how well the problem is represented.
6. Express the Railroad Crossing Gate Controller problem as a decision table. Discuss how well the problem is represented.
7. Express the Six-Coin Espresso Vending Machine (see Chapter 3) as a decision table. Compare your decision table to the one in the text of this chapter. Does the simplification make the decision table model any more useful?
8. Refer to Table 5.20 and develop both a customer-friendly and a greedy decision table for the second nine rules, in which a €0.50 coin is deposited. What can you say about half of the mixed-entry decision table when c3 is true (Yes)?
9. An extended-entry decision table can always be recast as a limited-entry decision table. The "third try" decision table for the NextDate problem (section 5.3.2.3) has three extended-entry conditions, one each for day, month, and year. There are five extended entries for Day, four for Month, and just one for Year. How many conditions will be in the equivalent limited-entry decision table? How many rules?
10. Are the "—" entries in Table 5.25 understood better as "don't care" or "must be false"?
11. What effect do the F! (must be false) entries in limited-entry decision tables have on rule consolidation? You might expand Table 5.25 into limited-entry decision table form, and then try to consolidate rules.

Chapter 6

Finite State Machines

Finite state machines have become a fairly standard notation for requirements specification. All the real-time extensions of structured analysis use some form of finite state machine, and nearly all forms of object-oriented analysis require either finite state machines or their extension, statecharts. Much of Section 6.1 is taken from *Software Testing: A Craftsman's Approach* (Jorgensen 2008).

6.1 Definition and Notation

A finite state machine is a directed graph (see Chapter 2) in which nodes are states and edges are transitions. Source and sink nodes become initial and terminal states, paths are modeled as paths, and so on. Most finite state machine notations add information to the edges (transitions) to indicate the cause of the transition and actions that occur as a result of the transition. Here is a formal definition.

Definition

A *finite state machine* is a 4-tuple (S, T, In, Out) where

    S is a set of states
    T is a set of transitions
    In is a set of inputs that cause transitions
    Out is a set of outputs that can occur on transitions

Figure 6.1 is a finite state machine for the Railroad Crossing Gate Controller.

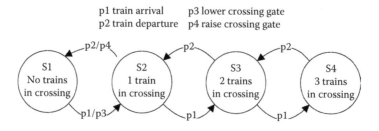

Figure 6.1   Finite state machine for the railroad crossing gate controller.

In the finite state machine in Figure 6.1, we have the following values for the 4-tuple:

S = {S1, S2, S3, S4}

T = {<S1, S2>, <S2, S3>, <S3, S4>, <S4, S3>, <S3, S2>, <S2, S1>}

In = {p1, p2}

Out = {p3, p4}

This machine contains four states and six transitions, which are shown as edges. The labels on the transitions follow a convention that the "numerator" is the event that causes the transition, and the "denominator" is the action that is associated with the transition. The transition from S1 to S2, for example, is caused by the input event p1 and generates the output event p3. Both p1 and p2 are context-sensitive input events. The response to these events depends on the context, expressed in this model as a state, in which the events occur. The events are mandatory—transitions do not just happen—but the actions are optional.

Paths through a finite state machine can be identified in three ways: as a sequence of states, as a sequence of state transitions, or as a sequence of events that cause transitions. A given finite state machine may represent a large number of distinct paths, much like the intention of a database represents many possible extensions (distinct populations). Regular expressions are a way to represent the "intention" of a finite state machine algebraically. Regular expressions have several popular notations:

- "Railroad Diagrams" (usually used to express programming language syntax
- BNF (interpreted either as Backus-Nauer Form or Backus Normal Form)
- Jackson Structure Diagrams

Each of these has three distinct features: sequence, selection (in the exclusive-or sense), and repetition. Here is a formal definition of a regular expression:

Definition

The *regular expressions over a set L* are defined recursively as follows:

The symbol Ø is a regular expression
The symbol x is a regular expression whenever x ∈ L
(A B), (A|B), and A* are regular expressions whenever A and B are regular
   expressions, where
   (A B) is the concatenation (sequence) of A followed by B
   (A|B) is the exclusive-or selection of A and B
A* is the repetition of A a finite number of times.

Now, suppose we take the set L to be the set of events that cause transitions in some finite state machine. Since transitions from any state are mutually exclusive, if we have an initial state and a terminal state, we can use a regular expression to describe all possible paths from the initial to the terminal state. In the finite state machine for the Railroad Crossing Gate Controller (Figure 6.1), there are only two events, p1 and p2. Assuming the initial state and the terminal states are both the one in which the intersection contains no trains, the regular expression will describe the infinite number of possible executions of the machine.

6.2 Technique

States are commonly used to represent any of the following:

■ Stages of processing
■ Data
■ Data conditions
■ Events that have occurred
■ Hardware configurations
■ Device status

Events that cause state transitions can be any of:

■ Input events
■ Data conditions
■ Passage of time
■ Logical combinations of the first three

Actions that are associated with transitions can be any of:

- Output events
- Changes in data values
- System actions/functions
- Logical combinations of the first three

Because finite state machines (FSMs) are directed graphs, it is common to represent them as we did with directed graphs: States are circles (or sometimes ovals) and transitions are arrows. A finite state machine can be completely represented textually by two tables: a transition table and an event table.

Definition

Given a finite state machine with m states and n input events, its *transition table* is an $m \times n$ matrix such that the entry in row i, column j refers to state i and event j. The value of the entry in position <i, j> is the state on which the transition caused by the event terminates.

Definition

Given a finite state machine with m states and n transitions, its *event table* is an m × n matrix such that the entry in row i, column j refers to state i and event j. The value of the entry in position <i, j> is the output event that occurs with the transition.

Tables 6.1 and 6.2 are the transition and event tables for the FSM in Figure 6.1. The event and transition tables are complementary: Neither can be derived from the other, and both are necessary to fully describe a finite state machine.

Finite state machines can be executed, but a few conventions are needed first. One is the notion of the active state. We sometimes speak of a system being "in" a certain state; when the system is modeled as a finite state machine, the active state refers to the state "we are in." A more precise way to understand a state is presented in the following definition.

Table 6.1   Transition Table for the Railroad Crossing Gate Controller FSM

	p1	p2
S1	S2	—
S2	S3	S1
S3	S4	S2
S4	—	S3

Table 6.2   Event Table for the Railroad Crossing Gate Controller FSM

	p1	p2
S1	p3	p4
S2	—	—
S3	—	—
S4	—	—

Definition

A *state* in a finite state machine is an interval of (execution) time during which a certain proposition is true.

In the Railroad Crossing Gate Controller example, the proposition for state S1 is

S1: There is no train in the intersection

If/when event p1 occurs, this state proposition is no longer true, so the time interval has ended, and the state proposition for state S2 becomes true. The "one state at a time" convention is nicely interpreted by saying that the state propositions are mutually exclusive.

Another convention is that finite state machines may have an initial state, which is the state that is active when a finite state machine is first entered. The initial state may be explicitly noted, or just described. One way to denote an initial state is to have a transition terminating in the initial state, but having no initial state. We also think of transitions as instantaneous occurrences, and the events that cause transitions also occur one at a time. To execute a finite state machine, we start with an initial state and provide a sequence of events that cause state transitions. As each event occurs, the transition changes the active state and a new event occurs. In this way, a sequence of events selects a path of states (or, equivalently, of transitions) through the machine. The close association among states, events, and transitions results in three common ways to describe a path:

- as a sequence of states,
- as a sequence of input events, or
- as a sequence of transitions.

Finite state machines might describe an infinite number of paths. Because the FSM in Figure 6.1 is 3-connected (see Chapter 2), it has an infinite number of paths. We sometimes speak of a path in a FSM as a scenario. Alternatively, paths can correspond to use cases, or even the user stories of agile development. In the

Railroad Crossing Gate Controller, the scenario—a train arrives, followed by a second train; a train departs, then the other train departs—has the state sequence <S1, S2, S3, S2, S1> and the event sequence <p1, p1, p2, p2>.

There are two additional facts about finite state machines:

1. There is no memory in a finite state machine.
2. The states are independent.

The "no memory" restriction means that the state propositions are truly independent, i.e., they have no memory of the truth or falsehood of other state propositions. The "independent states" restriction is closely related. The easiest way to understand it is that transitions emanating from a state cannot depend in any way on the history of "previous" states. In the example in Figure 6.1, the state propositions seem to have memory—the value of the number of trains in the intersection. This is both a common and a legitimate usage. It will be convenient to use this in the Espresso Vending Machine example to track the value of deposited coins. A situation that potentially violates these restrictions occurs in the Smart Fuel Pump problem. Suppose a transaction is paid for by a credit card. At the payment portion, how will the FSM know to send a transaction record to the credit card company? As a generality, when there are dependencies among states, paths that traverse dependent states are frequently impossible.

6.3 Continuing Examples

6.3.1 Simplified U.S. 1040EZ Income Tax Form

The Simplified U.S. 1040EZ Income Tax Form does not work well as a finite state machine. We can go through the motions by using states as stages of processing, as in Figure 6.2. The result is not as helpful as the flowchart in Chapter 4.

In Figure 6.2, some of the states are action oriented, not proposition oriented. Action-oriented states are a stylistic choice, and the state propositions would be something like "getting input values" and "computing AGI." The problem with action-oriented states is that transitions have a latent cause—usually completion of the action. Notice that a finite state machine with action-oriented states is an (unnecessary?) elaboration of a flowchart.

6.3.2 The NextDate Function

Even though there is a lot of decision making in the NextDate function, it also is poorly represented by a finite state machine (see Figure 6.3). As with the U.S. 1040EZ Income Tax Form, we have action-oriented states. Finite state machines do not support the identification of dependencies among equivalence classes of input variables, so in this sense, they are inferior to decision tables.

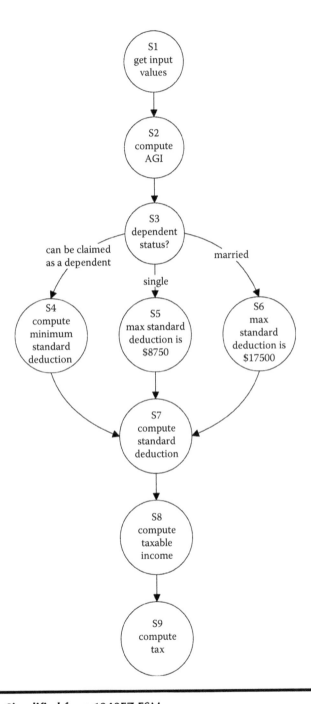

Figure 6.2   Simplified form 1040EZ FSM.

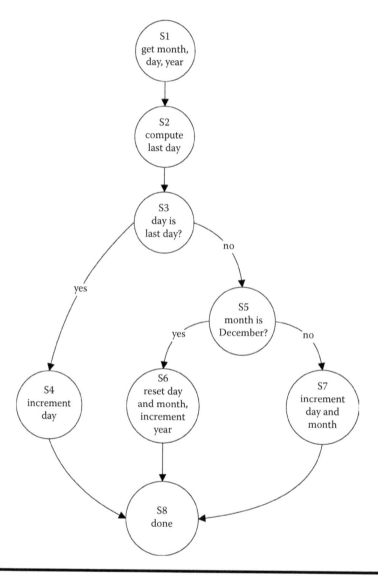

Figure 6.3 NextDate finite state machine.

6.3.3 Espresso Vending Machine

Because the espresso vending machine is an event-driven system, it is nicely represented with a finite state machine. In Figure 6.4, the names of the states serve as memory, thereby avoiding the "no memory" restriction.

Figures 6.4 and 6.5 show only prescribed behavior. Since the espresso machine is event driven, there is nothing to prohibit a user from inserting an overpayment.

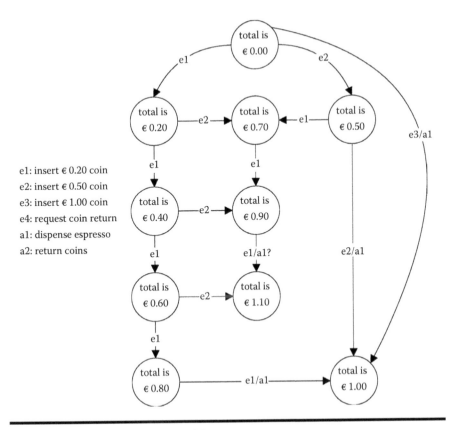

Figure 6.4 Espresso vending machine FSM.

This is (or should be) proscribed behavior. In the telephone switching system business, we referred to this as "abnormal subscriber behavior," and then we joked about
how many abnormal subscribers we had. But sometimes, it is necessary to defend
against abnormal behavior, and finite state machines make this possible. We simply
ask what are all the events that can occur in a given state, and then add transitions
for each of these events. The result often looks like the spaghetti FSM in Figure 6.6.
There are 44 transitions in Figure 6.6, so the improvement over a 54-rule decision
table is questionable.

The finite state machine in Figure 6.4 is almost identical to the decision table
in Chapter 5 (Table 5.20). One big difference is that the full decision table for
the espresso machine has 54 rules. The more concise finite state machine representation is certainly more helpful. Notice that the "request coin return" event
is missing. Since this is an event-driven system, it can occur in any state. If we
showed all these occurrences, we get the messy FSM in Figure 6.5. We will see
that the statechart notation simplifies this. To summarize, the finite state machine
model of the Espresso Vending Machine tells us more than the decision table. The

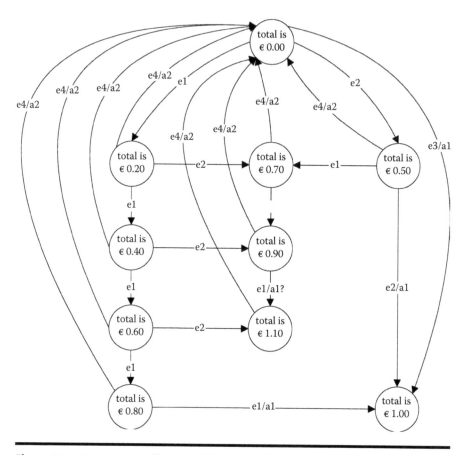

Figure 6.5 Espresso vending machine FSM with coin returns.

most important difference is that the decision table model is declarative: We cannot extract sequences of inputs that determine behavior.

Now the transition table (Table 6.3) may be a better modeling choice.

6.3.4 Smart Fuel Pump

In the preceding examples, we followed a top-down approach: Digest the narrative description, identify states and events and actions, then describe the state transitions. The Smart Fuel Pump problem works well with a bottom-up approach. We first identify local, device-oriented FSMs, and then compose these into successively higher level machines. Another approach might be to first identify all the events from the problem statement. We will combine these approaches. Many times, the simple state machines help us recognize events. Figure 6.7 shows three device-oriented finite state machines.

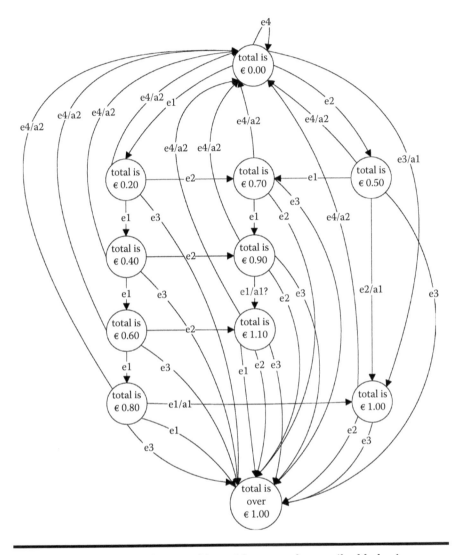

Figure 6.6 Espresso vending machine with pre- and proscribed behaviors.

Smart Fuel Pump Events

e1: attendant approve

e2: attendant reject

e3: credit card approve

e4: credit card reject

e5: select regular grade

e6: select mid-grade

e7: select premium grade

e8: squeeze trigger

e9: release trigger

e10: remove gun

e11: replace gun

e12: tank level below 4%

e13: customer ends fuel delivery

Table 6.3   Transition Table for the Espresso Vending Machine FSM in Figure 6.6

	e1	e2	e3	e4
S1 = total is €0.00	S2	S3	S9	S1
S2 = total is €0.20	S3	S7	S11	S1
S3 = total is €0.40	S4	S8	S11	S1
S4 = total is €0.60	S5	S10	S11	S1
S5 = total is €0.80	S6	S11	S11	S1
S6 = total is €0.50	S7	S11	S11	S1
S7 = total is €0.70	S8	S11	S11	S1
S8 = total is €0.90	S10	S11	S11	S1
S9 = total is €1.00	S11	S11	S11	S1
S10 = total is €1.10	S11	S11	S11	S1
S11 = total is over €1.00	...	...	...	...

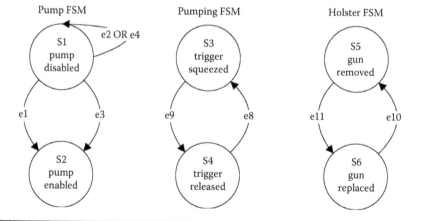

Figure 6.7   Three device-oriented finite state machines.

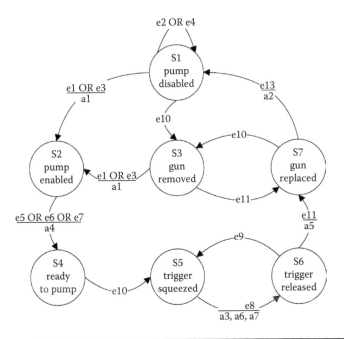

Figure 6.8   Composite smart fuel pump finite state machine.

We gradually build a more complex FSM by composing the device-oriented FSMs (see Figure 6.8).

Smart Fuel Pump Actions

a1: start pump motor	a5: free pump clutch
a2: stop pump motor	a6: update volume pumped display
a3: engage pump clutch	a7: update transaction cost display
a4: reset displays	

The last step is to show the (low probability) effect of event e12: tank level below 4% (see Figure 6.9). This can occur at any point in a customer transaction, so as with the Espresso Vending Machine FSM, we will have many additional transitions. There is another, very subtle problem: If the customer selects credit card payment, there should be a transaction record sent to the credit card company when the transaction ends. The problem is that this does not happen if the transaction is attendant approved. This requires memory. A very cumbersome way to avoid the problem is to duplicate all of the states except for S1, where half refer to attendant approval and the other half to credit card approval. (Then the e1 OR e3 cause of the transition from S1 to S2 is also split.) Note that this independent consideration almost doubles the size of the FSM—another instance of Jorgensen's First Law of Software Engineering.

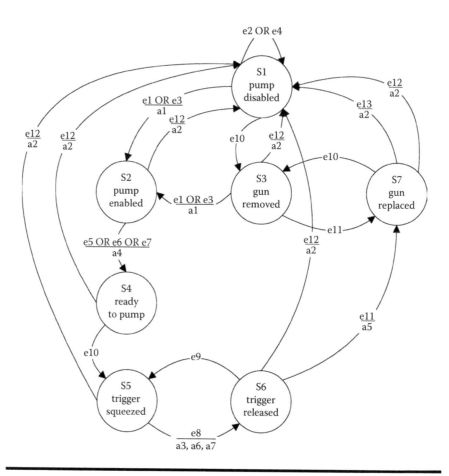

Figure 6.9   Smart fuel pump FSM with tank-level event.

The finite state machine model of the Smart Fuel Pump problem is a quantum improvement over the flowchart and decision table models. The main difference—sequences of behavior are visually obvious, and hence, can be moved into test cases. There are several examples of the structural primitives: Sequence is seen in successive states, selection when different events cause two (or more) transitions from a single state, and repetition when two states are in a loop, as with the trigger squeeze and release states.

There are also some Extended Systems Modeling Language (ESML) prompts directly modeled in the finite state machine. The attendant and credit card approvals are both ESML Enable prompts, and if either rejects the transaction, we have ESML Disable. The 4% tank-level event is an ESML Suspend that occurs in many states (this will be very elegant in the statechart model). Finally, the squeeze trigger event, accidentally per its name, is an ESML Trigger for the price and fuel quantity display processes.

There are no interesting context-sensitive input events, nor are there multiple-context output events. There are clear points of event quiescence, for example, when the trigger is released. Normally these points would be governed by a timeout event, but that is (deliberately) not in the problem statement.

6.3.5 *Saturn Windshield Wiper Controller*

There are two independent devices in the Saturn Windshield Wiper Controller: the lever and the dial. The input and output events are:

e1: move lever up one position   e2: move lever down one position
e3: move dial up one position   e4: move dial down one position

a1: deliver 0 wipes per minute   a2: deliver 6 wipes per minute
a3: deliver 12 wipes per minute   a4: deliver 20 wipes per minute
a5: deliver 30 wipes per minute   a6: deliver 60 wipes per minute

The two device-oriented FSMs are shown in Figure 6.10. Notice the question mark actions on every transition in the Dial FSM and on the transitions to state S2

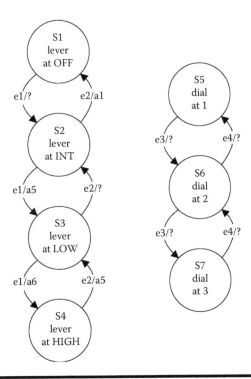

Figure 6.10   Lever and dial finite state machines.

in the Lever FSM. These actions are all undetermined because neither FSM knows the active state of the other. Secondly, event e1 is a context-sensitive input event; the response is different depending on the context in which event e1 occurs.

The lever events are a good example of a subtlety about events. We could replace event "e1: move lever up one position" with three more specific events:

e.1.1: move lever Off to Int
e.1.2: move lever Int to Low
e.1.3: move lever Low to High

This choice is tantamount to moving the context of a context-sensitive input event into a set of more specific input events. In a similar way, multiple-context output events can be made more specific. The choice between context sensitivity and more specific events is really one of style. If the state machines are used to automatically generate test cases, the more specific version of events is preferred.

Our next step is to remove the ambiguity of transition actions. Figure 6.11 shows a brute force way—simply take the Cartesian product of the two FSMs.

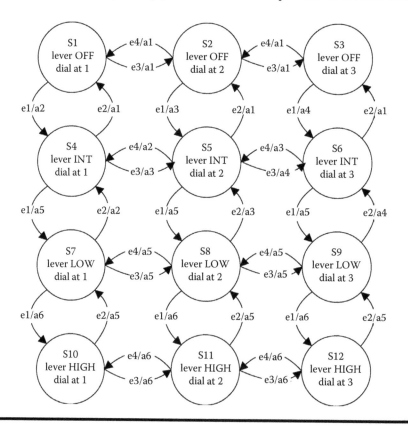

Figure 6.11   Cartesian product of the lever and dial FSMs.

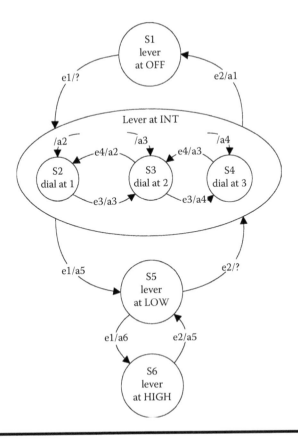

Figure 6.12   Hierarchical FSM for the Saturn windshield wiper.

There is much redundancy in Figure 6.11: The triples of horizontal states (in which the Lever position is constant) are only interesting when the lever is in the INT (intermittent) state. This is not nearly as elegant as the extended-entry decision table with the Don't Care entries in Table 5.25, and it certainly will not scale up well for devices with more states. (Jorgensen's First Law of Software Engineering strikes again!)

There are two possible remedies for the mess in Figure 6.11. One is to use a notion of hierarchy, as in Figure 6.12. The other is to use communicating finite state machines, sometimes abbreviated as CFMs. Full treatment involves more formalism than most of us need, so for now, we just use the notion of a message. (Use of messages in CFMs probably predates the use of messages in object-oriented programming.) Rather than a true output action on a transition, a CFM can just send a message to another finite state machine. (We shall see exactly this mechanism in statecharts.) The messages from the Dial FSM to

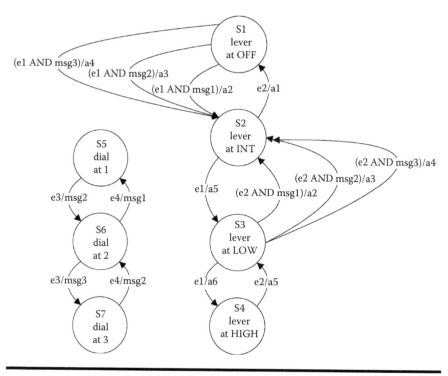

Figure 6.13   Lever and dial FSMs as communicating finite state machines.

the Lever FSM just provide the position of the Dial (1, 2, or 3). In Figure 6.13, the messages are:

    msg1: dial at 1
    msg2: dial at 2
    msg3: dial at 3

Figure 6.13 almost completely resolves the ambiguity we had in Figure 6.10. The only remaining question has to do with event quiescence: What if no event occurs in the Dial FSM? If no dial event occurs, no message will be sent to the Lever FSM. Thus once the Lever FSM is in either state S1 or S3, it is stuck there until a dial event occurs. The actual answer in "pure communicating finite state machines" is that, because both FSMs are in communication, each always knows the active state of the other. We will see an even clearer expression of this in Chapter 9 on statecharts. In fact, the transitions to states S2, S3, and S4 in Figure 6.12 borrow some transition notation from statecharts.

6.4 Finite State Machine Engines

Recall that the basic structure of a finite state machine consists of (S, T, In, Out), where

S is a set of states
T is a set of transitions
In is a set of inputs that cause transitions
Out is a set of outputs that can occur on transitions

Each of these elements is needed in a finite state machine execution engine. A likely implementation consists of a graphical user interface (GUI) in which the set of states is given, and the set of events (and other conditions, if needed) is available, probably via a drop-down menu. Once an initial state is identified (interactively, by the customer/user), the user can "cause" an event to occur, thereby generating a transition to the next state. If actions occur on the transition, they are noted. The customer/user can move from state to state by selecting events. One interesting possibility is that the user is free to select events that correspond to proscribed behavior, such as paying too much for an espresso.

A finite state machine engine would produce an execution table similar to the one in Table 6.4 for the typical use case below.

Table 6.4   Execution Table for the Saturn Windshield Wiper Controller

Step	In States	Input Event	Next States	Output Action [a]
1	Off, 1	e1: move lever up one position	Int, 1	a2: deliver 6 wpm
2	Int, 1	e3: move dial up one position	Int, 2	a3: deliver 10 wpm
3	Int, 2	e1: move lever up one position	Low, 2	a5: deliver 30 wpm
4	Low, 2	e1: move lever up one position	High, 2	a6: deliver 60 wpm
5	High, 2	e2: move lever down one position	Low, 2	a5: deliver 30 wpm
6	Low, 2	e3: move dial up one position	Low, 3	a5: deliver 30 wpm
7	Low, 3	e2: move lever down one position	Int, 3	a4: deliver 20 wpm
8	Int, 3	e2: move lever down one position	Off, 3	a1: deliver 0 wpm

[a] wpm = wipes per minute.

Use Case Name:	Saturn Windshield Wiper Controller Execution Table Example	
Use Case ID:	SWWC-1	
Description:	Operator moves through a typical sequence of lever and dial events	
Preconditions:	1. Lever position is OFF, Dial position is 1	
Event Sequence:	**Input Event**	**System Response**
	1. e1: move lever up one position	2. a2: deliver 6 wipes per minute
	3. e3: move dial up one position	4. a3: deliver 10 wipes per minute
	5. e1: move lever up one position	6. a5: deliver 10 wipes per minute
	7. e1: move lever up one position	8. a6: deliver 10 wipes per minute
	9. e2: move lever down one position	10. a5: deliver 10 wipes per minute
	11. e3: move dial up one position	...
	12. e2: move lever down one position	13. a4: deliver 20 wipes per minute
	14. e2: move lever down one position	15. a1: deliver 0 wipes per minute
Postconditions:	1. Lever position is OFF, Dial position is 3	

6.5 Advantages and Limitations

Finite state machines are intuitively understandable by both developers and customers. When displayed in graphical form, paths are easily seen, and since this is a two-dimensional representation, parallelism can be identified visually. Since finite state machines can express both prescribed and proscribed behaviors, they are especially amenable to analysis by execution engines. Also, finite state machines can be extended by associating probabilities with transitions. Doing so yields a notion of execution-time traffic behavior, which, in turn, supports the notion of operational profiles in system testing. Finally, if cost penalties can be associated with paths, the costs and probabilities will support risk-based testing.

Table 6.5 Representation of Behavioral Issues with Finite State Machines

Issue	Represented?	Comments/Example
Sequence	yes	...
Selection	awkward	Must use alternative events to cause distinct transitions
Repetition	yes	...
Enable	no	The attendant or credit card approval; also the trigger squeeze event enables the display process
Disable	no	The 4% level event; also the trigger release event disables the display process
Trigger	no	The trigger squeeze event triggers the flow of fuel
Activate	no	The enable and disable primitives combine to be an activate
Suspend	no	The trigger release event could be interpreted as an ESML Suspend, because the subsequent trigger squeeze event resumes the display processes where they left off
Resume	no	The trigger squeeze event could be interpreted as an ESML Resume, because the display processes where they left off
Pause	no	The suspend and resume prompts combine to be an ESML Pause
Conflict	no	...
Priority	no	...
Mutual exclusion	no	...
Concurrent execution	no	Must allocate FSMs to separate devices
Deadlock	no	Observed in an execution table
Context-sensitive input events	yes	The coin insertion events in the espresso vending machine

(Continued)

Table 6.5   Representation of Behavioral Issues with Finite State Machines (Continued)

Issue	Represented?	Comments Example
Multiple-context output events	yes	The dispense espresso event in the espresso vending machine
Asynchronous events	no	Depends on execution table
Event quiescence	no	Depends on marking sequence; it occurs after a trigger release event

On the downside, Table 6.5 shows that many behavioral issues cannot be represented in finite state machines. Even worse, finite state machines are inherently vulnerable to the famous state machine explosion. We saw an example of this in Figure 6.6, with all the paths due to an event occurring in many states. Another classical example is a finite state machine description of an elevator system in a building. A former student modeled a building with nine floors and three elevators. The resulting finite state machine had over 110,000 distinct states. (And no, he didn't provide a diagram!) Here, the explosion was due to the multiplying effect of many truly independent aspects of the problem.

References

Jorgensen, Paul C. 2008. *Software testing: A craftsman's approach.* 3rd ed. New York: Taylor and Francis.

Exercises

1. Find examples of finite state machines in noncomputing situations. Discuss how effectively they communicate the problem being addressed.
2. Express the Windchill Factor Table problem as a finite state machine. Discuss how well the problem is represented.
3. Express the Previous Date problem as a finite state machine. Discuss how well the problem is represented.
4. Express the Saturn Cruise Control problem as a finite state machine. Discuss how well the problem is represented.
5. Express the Programmable Thermostat problem as a finite state machine. Discuss how well the problem is represented.
6. Express the Railroad Crossing Gate Controller problem as a finite state machine. Discuss how well the problem is represented.
7. Express the Six-Coin Espresso Vending Machine (see Chapter 3) as a finite state machine. Compare your finite state machine to the one in the text. Does the simplification make the finite state machine model any more useful?
8. Consider the pumping portion of the Smart Fuel Pump that begins with the event e10: remove gun, followed by an arbitrary number of trigger-squeeze and -release events (e8 and e9) and ended with e11: replace gun. Make the regular expression for this portion of the problem.

Chapter 7

Petri Nets

Petri nets were the topic of Carl Adam Petri's Ph.D. dissertation in 1963; today they are the accepted model for protocols and event-driven applications.

7.1 Definition and Notation

Petri nets are a special form of directed graph: a bipartite directed graph. (A bipartite graph has two sets of nodes, V_1 and V_2, and a set of edges E, with the restriction that every edge has its initial node on one of the sets V_1, V_2, and its terminal node in the other set.) In a Petri net, one of the sets is referred to as "places," and the other is referred to as "transitions." These sets are usually denoted as P and T, respectively. Places are inputs to and outputs of transitions; the input and output relationships are functions, and they are usually denoted as In and Out, as in the following definition.

Definition

A *Petri net* is a bipartite-directed graph (P, T, In, Out) in which P and T are disjoint sets of nodes, and In and Out are sets of edges, where In $\subseteq$ P $\times$ T, and Out $\subseteq$ T $\times$ P.

For the sample Petri net in Figure 7.1, the sets P, T, In, and Out are:

$$P = \{p1, p2, p3, p4, p5\}$$

$$T = \{t1, t2, t3\}$$

$$In = \{<p1, t1>, <p5, t1>, <p5, t3>, <p2, t3>, <p3, t2>\}$$

$$Out = \{<t1, p3>, <t2, p4>, <t3, p4>\}$$

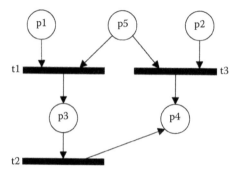

Figure 7.1   A Petri net.

Places are usually drawn as circles and transitions as rectangular bars. In Europe, transitions are frequently depicted as open rectangles. Petri nets are executable in more interesting ways than finite state machines (FSMs). The next few definitions lead us to Petri net execution.

Definition

A *marked Petri net* is a 5-tuple (P, T, In, Out, M) in which (P, T, In, Out) is a Petri net and M is a set of mappings of places to positive integers.

The set M is called the marking set of the Petri net. Elements of M are *n*-tuples, where n is the number of places in the set P. For the Petri net in Figure 7.1, the set M contains elements of the form <*n1, n2, n3, n4, n5*>, where the *n*'s are the integers associated with the respective places. The number associated with a place refers to the number of tokens that are said to be "in" the place. Tokens are abstractions that can be interpreted in modeling situations. For example, tokens might refer to the number of times a place has been used, or the number of things in a place, or whether the place is true. Figure 7.2 shows a marked Petri net. The marking tuple for the marked Petri net in Figure 7.2 is <1, 1, 0, 2, 0>. We need the concept of tokens to make two essential definitions.

7.1.1 Transition Enabling and Firing

Definition

A transition in a Petri net is *enabled* if there is at least one token in each of its input places.

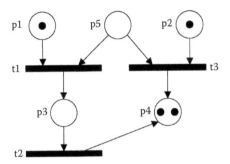

Figure 7.2   A marked Petri net.

There are no enabled transitions in the marked Petri net in Figure 7.2. If we put a token in place p3, then transition t2 would be enabled.

Definition

When an enabled Petri net transition *fires*, one token is removed from each of its input places, and one token is added to each of its output places.

In Figure 7.3, transition t2 is enabled in the upper net, and it has been fired in the lower net. The marking set for the net in Figure 7.3 contains two tuples, the first shows the net when t2 is enabled, and the second shows the net after t2 has fired.

$$M = \{<1, 1, 1, 2, 0>, <1, 1, 0, 3, 0>\}$$

Tokens may be created or destroyed by transition firings. Under special conditions, the total number of tokens in a net never changes; such nets are called conservative. We usually won't worry about token conservation. Markings let us execute Petri nets in much the same way that we execute finite state machines. (In fact, finite state machines are a special case of Petri nets.) Some formulations of Petri nets associate a weight with each input edge to a transition. The weight, a natural number, signifies the number of tokens that must be in the input place in order for that place to contribute to enabling. Similarly, there can be a weight on an output edge that signifies how many tokens are placed in an output place when the transition fires. We will not make use of these extensions.

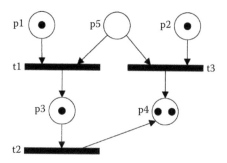

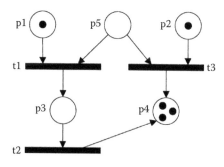

Figure 7.3 Before and after firing t2.

7.1.2 Petri Net Conflict

Suppose we had a different marking of the net in Figure 7.3; in this new marking, places p1, p2, and p5 are all marked. With such a marking, transitions t1 and t3 are both enabled. If we choose to fire transition t1, the token in place p5 is removed, and t3 is no longer enabled. Similarly, if we choose to fire t3, we disable t1. This pattern is known as Petri net conflict; more specifically, we say that transitions t1 and t3 are in conflict with respect to place p5. Petri net conflict exhibits an interesting form of interaction between two transitions.

7.1.3 The Producer–Consumer Problem

The Producer–Consumer problem is a Petri net classic. In Figure 7.4, nodes p1, p2, and p3 and transitions t1 and t2 represent the producer. My favorite interpretation is Mom baking chocolate chip cookies (one at a time, as we shall see), and a father and son each contending for cookies. Consumer 1 (the father) is represented by nodes p3, p4, and p5 and transitions t3 and t4. Similarly, Consumer 2 is represented by nodes p3, p6, and p7 and transitions t5 and t6.

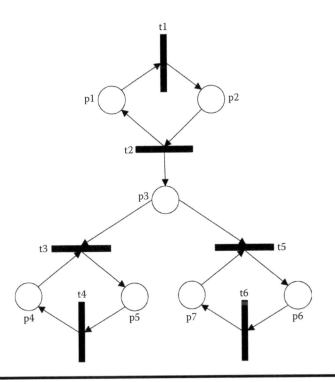

Figure 7.4 Producer-consumer Petri net.

Possible interpretations of the places and transitions are:

p1: request to bake
p2: ready to bake
p3: cookie ready to be eaten
p4, p7: ready for another cookie
p5, p6: consumer has a cookie

t1: putting cookie dough on pan
t2: baking cookie
t3, t5: consumer takes one cookie
t4, t6: consumer eats cookie

Figure 7.5 shows a possible initial marking for the Producer–Consumer Petri net.

Table 7.1 describes a scenario in the Producer–Consumer problem in which the producer bakes a cookie (at m0); consumers 1 and 2 are in Petri net conflict over the cookie (at m1); consumer 2 takes the cookie (firing t5 at step m1); and the producer prepares to bake another cookie (at step m2), and bakes on (at step m3). At this point, only consumer 1 is enabled, and takes the just-baked cookie (at step m4). In the last step (of this scenario), the producer is ready to bake another cookie and consumer 2 is still waiting.

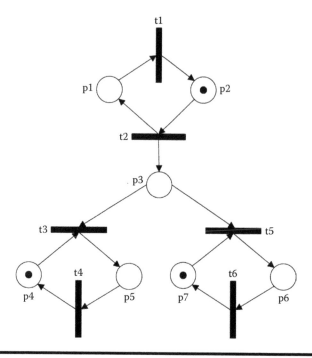

Figure 7.5   Possible initial marking for the producer-consumer Petri net.

This particular form of basic Petri nets is known as a "free choice" net, because when more than one transition is enabled, someone (the customer/user!) makes a choice of which transition to fire. There is extensive commercial-tool support for this form of Petri net execution, so this is clearly an executable specification. There are seven distinct levels of Petri net execution (see Section 7.5).

Table 7.1   A Sample Execution Table of the Producer–Consumer Petri Net

Execution Step	Marking	Enabled Transitions	Fired Transition
m0	<0, 1, 0, 1, 0, 0, 1>	t2	t2
m1	<1, 0, 1, 1, 0, 0, 1>	t1, t3, t5	t5
m2	<1, 0, 0, 1, 0, 0, 1>	t1, t6	t1
m3	<0, 1, 0, 1, 0, 1, 0>	t2, t6	t2
m4	<1, 0, 1, 1, 0, 1, 0>	t1, t3, t6	t3
m5	<1, 0, 0, 0, 1, 1, 0>	t1, t6	

7.2 Technique

Because Petri nets are less well understood, we will look extensively at questions of technique. For starters, here are some general hints:

1. Use transitions to represent actions.
2. Use places to represent any of the following:
   - Data
   - Pre- and postconditions
   - States
   - Messages
   - Events
3. Use the Input relationship to represent prerequisites and inputs.
4. Use the Output relationship to represent consequences and outputs.
5. Use markings to represent "states" of a net, memory, or counters.
6. Tasks can be considered to be individual transitions or subnets.
7. Subsets of input places to a transition can be used to define a context.

In the following subsections, we look at Petri net formulations of the modeling issues identified in Table 3.2.

7.2.1 Sequence, Selection, and Repetition

Sequence and repetition are easily shown in a Petri net (see Figure 7.6). Transitions s1 and s2 are in sequence, and they are also in a loop.

Selection is not as simple. Basically, there are two choices, as shown in Figure 7.7, which refers to part of the Simplified U.S. 1040EZ Income Tax Form.

In the upper Petri net, the actual selection is made by which place is marked, p1 or p2 (they are in an exclusive-or relation). The transitions s1 and s2 perform

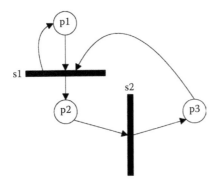

Figure 7.6   Sequence and repetition in a Petri net.

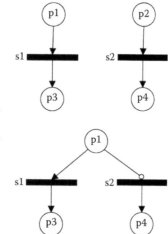

p1: taxpayer is married
p2: taxpayer is single
p3: maximum standard deduction = $10700
p4: maximum standard deduction = $5350
s1: compute deduction for a married person
s2: compute deduction for a single person

Figure 7.7 Two forms of Petri net selection.

the simple calculation, and leave the results in places p3 and p4. The lower net uses an "inhibitor arc," which is denoted by a little circle at the end rather than an arrowhead. Inhibitor arcs contribute to transition enabling in a negative way: If the place is not marked, the inhibitor arc helps enable the transition to which it is connected. So if p1 refers to the condition "taxpayer is married," marking place p1 is interpreted as the proposition p1 being true, and no marking refers to p1 being false. Which form of selection is better is really a personal, stylistic choice. I prefer the simpler alternative (as in the upper part of Figure 7.7).

7.2.2 Enable, Disable, and Activate

These were originally defined as prompts in the Extended Systems Modeling Language by the ESML group (Bruyn 1988). The natural-language definitions are:

Definition

> *Enable*: When activity A enables activity B, activity B may execute, but not necessarily immediately.
> *Disable*: When activity A disables activity B, activity B may not execute. The termination is immediate, which makes Disable look like an "untrigger" (defined soon).
> *Activate*: An enable/disable sequence performed by activity A for/on activity B. Presumably there is a time interval in which B does what it has been enabled to do.

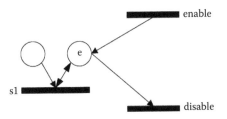

Figure 7.8 Petri nets for enable, disable, and activate.

The task s1 in Figure 7.8 cannot fire unless it has been enabled by the enable task. Once s1 is enabled, it reenables itself every time it fires. The disable task is in Petri net conflict with s1 with respect to the enable place. If the disable transition fires, s1 is disabled.

7.2.3 Trigger

Trigger is another ESML prompt, defined as:

Definition

Trigger: When activity A triggers activity B, B immediately executes.

Task s1 in Figure 7.9 is partially enabled. When the trigger transition fires, the trigger place is marked, and then s1 can fire.

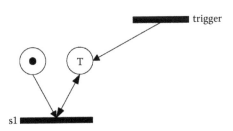

Figure 7.9 Petri net for the ESML trigger.

7.2.4 Suspend, Resume, and Pause

More ESML prompts:

Definition

Suspend: When activity A suspends activity B, activity B no longer executes, but intermediate work is saved.

Resume: When activity A resumes, activity B (which has been suspended) starts with the partially completed work that was in progress when it was suspended.

Pause: This is a suspend/resume sequence performed by activity A for/on activity B. Presumably there is a time interval in which B does nothing.

The intent of the ESML Suspend and Resume prompts is that they interrupt an executing task, and then restart it "where it left off." Task s1 is subdivided into three (an arbitrary choice) subtasks, as shown in Figure 7.10 to illustrate the "where it left off" part of the problem. Notice that the suspend transition has an interlock with the resume transition, so the suspend transition must fire first. The suspend transition is in Petri net conflict with some input to an intermediate task. Firing the suspend transition disables the intermediate subtask (s1.2 here), and firing the resume transition reenables s1.2.

The ESML Activate prompt is just an enable-disable sequence; similarly, the ESML Pause prompt is just a suspend-resume sequence.

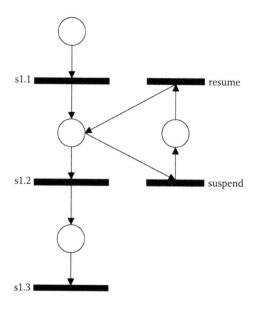

Figure 7.10   Petri net for ESML suspend, resume, and pause.

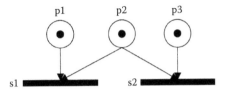

Figure 7.11 Petri net conflict.

7.2.5 Conflict and Priority

Both tasks s1 and s2 are enabled in Figure 7.11. Firing either one disables the other. This is the classic form of Petri net conflict. One way to break a conflict is to use an interlock place that forces task s2 to wait until task s1 has fired, as in Figure 7.12.

7.2.6 Mutual Exclusion

In Figure 7.13, the sequence <t1.1, t1.2, t1.3> and the sequence <t2.1, t2.2, t2.3> are mutually exclusive. Because t1.1 and t2.1 are in Petri net conflict with the semaphore place (S), firing one disables the other, and the exclusion is continued until the end of the excluded region (at either t1.3 or t2.3). Notice that the semaphore can be understood as a "bidirectional interlock."

7.2.7 Synchronization

Tasks 1, 2, and 3 are given a simultaneous start by the "start" task in Figure 7.14. To be truly parallel, the tasks would have to be in separate devices; this is not shown in the Petri net. This is sometimes described as a synchronized start.

In the lower part of Figure 7.14, the "stop" task cannot execute until each of its prerequisite tasks (tasks 1, 2, and 3) is complete. The Two-Phase Commit protocol for updates in a distributed database is a sequence of the synchronized starts and stops shown in Figure 7.14.

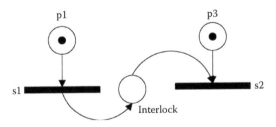

Figure 7.12 Petri net interlock.

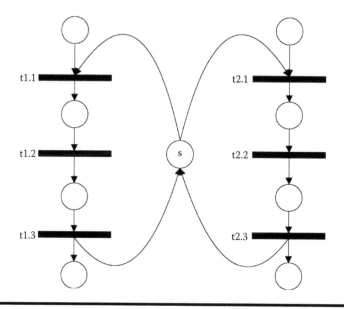

Figure 7.13 Petri net for mutual exclusion.

7.2.8 Some Consequences of Marking and Enabling

Marking places in a Petri net is a graphical/numerical way to represent various possible execution sequences of an unmarked Petri net. In Figure 7.15, we revisit the producer portion of the Producer–Consumer problem in Figure 7.4.

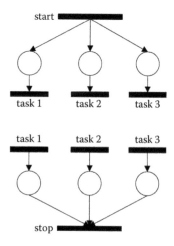

Figure 7.14 Synchronized start and stop.

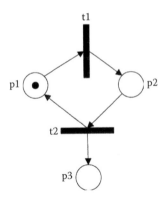

Figure 7.15   The producer Petri net.

Since place p1 is marked, transition t1 is enabled. If we fire t1, place p1 is no longer marked, but place p2 is marked. Now transition t2 is enabled. If we fire t2, place p2 is no longer marked, but places p1 and p3 are marked. We could continue firing t1 and t2, and after each cycle, p3 would have an additional marking token. Table 7.2 shows a few time steps of this.

First observation: Either t1 or t2 is always enabled, so we could execute this Petri net without limit.

Definition

A *live* Petri net is one in which some transition is always enabled.

Liveness depends on the initial marking. In our example, if the initial marking was just p3, no transition would be enabled.

Table 7.2   A Sample Execution Table of the Producer Petri Net

Execution Step	Marking <p1, p2, p3>	Enabled Transitions	Fired Transition
m0	<1, 0, 0>	t1	t1
m1	<0, 1, 0>	t2	t2
m2	<1, 0, 1>	t1	t1
m3	<0, 1, 1>	t2	t2
m4	<1, 0, 2>	t1	t1
m5	<0, 1, 2>	t2	t2

Definition

In a Petri net, *deadlock* occurs when no transition is enabled.

If we removed place p3 from the Petri net in Figure 7.15, there would always be exactly one token in the live net. When the total number of tokens is conserved, we say the net is conservative.

Definition

A Petri net is *conservative* if the sum of all tokens in the net is constant.

7.3 Examples

The variable names and other notation used in these figures are taken from those defined in Chapter 3.

7.3.1 Simplified U.S. 1040EZ Income Tax Form

At first, it would seem that a Petri net formulation (see Figure 7.16) is technical overkill; however, there is an interesting benefit of the Petri net that is not easily derived from the flowchart formulation. If there is an error somewhere in the series of calculations, the path of inputs, outputs, and transitions can be followed back to the true inputs. (Incidentally, true inputs are always places with indegree = 0; similarly, true outputs always have outdegree = 0.) For example, if the computed tax were too high, it could be traced back to the inputs described by places—p1, p2, p3, p4, and p5. Also, note that both forms of selection are used in Figure 7.16.

7.3.2 The NextDate Function

In this example, we will see how the intensive decisional logic in the NextDate function can be handled by initial markings. If the month is February, transitions s1 and s2 are in conflict. The marking of p2 and p3 resolves the conflict. Similarly, whether the month has 30 or 31 days, either s3 or s4 is enabled. Since p2 and p3 are mutually exclusive, and also p1, p4, p5, and p6 are mutually exclusive, only one of transitions s1, s2, s3, and s4 will be enabled. This is guaranteed by logically correct initial markings. There is a subtle problem with places p8 and p9: They are shown as true inputs, but how can they have a value if the value of the lastDay (p7) has not been computed? The Petri net formulation shows more of the sequential nature of NextDate, and some of the potential parallel computing, but overall, the decision table formulation is clearer, and obviously simpler (see Figure 7.17).

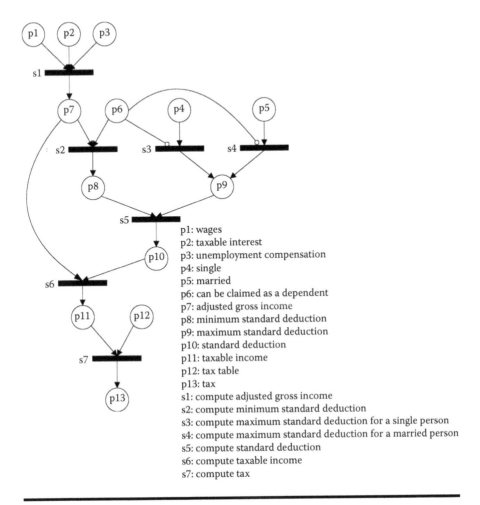

p1: wages
p2: taxable interest
p3: unemployment compensation
p4: single
p5: married
p6: can be claimed as a dependent
p7: adjusted gross income
p8: minimum standard deduction
p9: maximum standard deduction
p10: standard deduction
p11: taxable income
p12: tax table
p13: tax
s1: compute adjusted gross income
s2: compute minimum standard deduction
s3: compute maximum standard deduction for a single person
s4: compute maximum standard deduction for a married person
s5: compute standard deduction
s6: compute taxable income
s7: compute tax

Figure 7.16 Petri net of the U.S. 1040EZ Form.

7.3.3 *Espresso Vending Machine*

This is a good place to cover two more Petri net topics. The first is that a finite state machine is a special case of a Petri net (see Figure 7.18). To make a Petri net out of a finite state machine, consider the states to be places, and the transition to be a Petri net transition. This is an oversimplification, because the transitions in an FSM are caused by something, and can generate outputs. In FSM notation, this is the "fraction" that annotates a state transition.

The FSM in the upper left part of Figure 7.18 is taken from the Espresso Vending Machine FSM in Chapter 6. The simpler transformation to a Petri net

p1: February   p2: common year
p3: leap year   p4: 30-day month
p5: 31-day month   p6: December
p7: lastDay   p8: day < last day?
p9: day = last day?   p10: NextDate computed
s1: set last day = 28   s2: set last day = 29
s3: set last day = 30   s4: set last day = 31
s5: increment day, no change to month and year
s6: reset day to 1, increment month
s7: reset day and month to 1, increment year

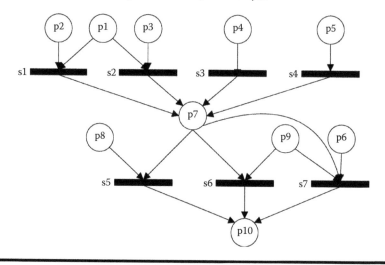

Figure 7.17   Petri net of the NextDate function.

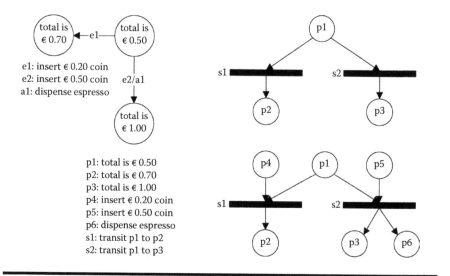

e1: insert € 0.20 coin
e2: insert € 0.50 coin
a1: dispense espresso

p1: total is € 0.50
p2: total is € 0.70
p3: total is € 1.00
p4: insert € 0.20 coin
p5: insert € 0.50 coin
p6: dispense espresso
s1: transit p1 to p2
s2: transit p1 to p3

Figure 7.18   Converting FSMs to Petri nets.

p1: total is € 0.00
p2: total is € 0.20
p3: total is € 0.40
p4: total is € 0.60
p5: total is € 0.80
p6: total is € 1.00
p7: total is € 0.50
p8: total is € 0.70
p9: total is € 0.90
p10: total is € 1.10
p11: insert € 0.20 coin
p12: insert € 0.50 coin
p13: insert € 1.00 coin
p14: request coin return
p15: dispense espresso
p16: return coins

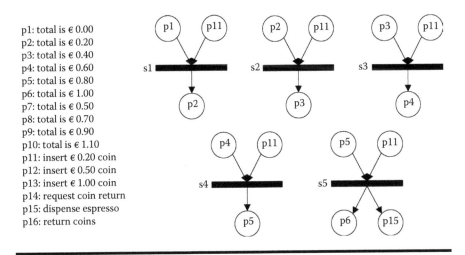

Figure 7.19 Transition-level Petri nets for the Espresso Vending Machine.

is the upper right figure, but it is misleading. It looks like a synchronized start of transitions s1 and s2, and this is clearly incorrect. If we add places to represent the FSM transition annotations, we see that, as in the lower right Petri net, we actually have transitions s1 and s2 in conflict with respect to place p1. The events p4 and p5 resolve the conflict.

The second topic concerns a bottom-up approach to developing a full Petri net. We can begin with Petri nets of parts of a problem, and compose them into larger nets. This partially solves the problem of scaling up to larger applications. Figure 7.19 contains several Petri nets of the Espresso Vending Machine; the transitions correspond to FSM state transitions.

If we look carefully, we see that the output of s1 is an input to s2, the output of s2 is an input to s3, and so on. We can compose these into a sequence <s1, s2, s3, s4, s5>, five insertions of a €0.20 coin, as in Figure 7.20. The composition in Figure 7.20 has a clear initial place, p1, and also shows that p11 can/should occur five times. Also, note the extensive enabling in Figure 7.20: When s1 fires, it enables s2; when s2 fires, it enables s3, and so on.

Composing individual Petri nets can be tricky. We could have composed the individual nets with respect to place p11 (inserting a €0.20 coin); after all, this does occur in each state p1, p2, p3, p4, and p5. We would have the net in Figure 7.21, but now, there is no obvious initial marking, and it appears that p11 only occurs once.

Another possibility is to remove as much redundancy as possible, in effect combining Figures 7.20 and 7.21 into Figure 7.22. Figure 7.22 has a certain minimalist elegance, but it still appears that p11 only occurs once. Of course, we could mark

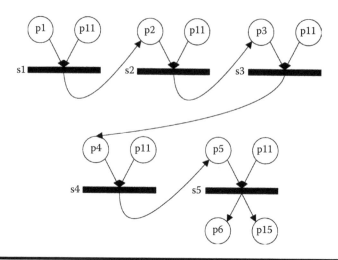

Figure 7.20   Composing Petri nets.

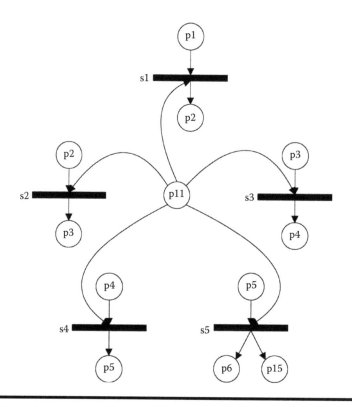

Figure 7.21   Composing with respect to p11.

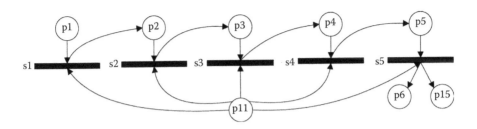

Figure 7.22   Composing to eliminate all redundant places.

it with five initial tokens, and that might help. We shall see that this ambiguity is resolved by event-driven Petri nets in Chapter 8.

Meanwhile, back at the Espresso Vending Machine problem, we have only modeled the part that deals with the €0.20 coin. What about the other coins? And what about the "return coins" event? The portion dealing with the €0.50 coin is so close to what we have done so far, it is left as an exercise. The coin-return event is much more interesting, since it can occur in any state, as shown in Figure 7.23. It should be clear

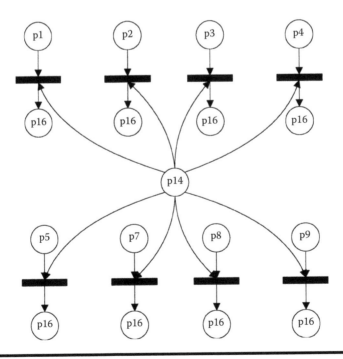

Figure 7.23   Composition with respect to the coin-return event.

Table 7.3 Input and Output Relations for Figure 7.20

Input			Output	
Place	Transition		Transition	Place
p1	s1		s1	p2
p2	s2		s2	p3
p3	s3		s3	p4
p4	s4		s4	p5
p5	s5		s5	p6
p11	s1		s5	p15
p11	s2			
p11	s3			
p11	s4			
p11	s5			

that there are practical limits to Petri net composition. Even in this small example, if we did the full net, we would be back to the graphical equivalent of spaghetti code. Fortunately, there is an elegant resolution using an idea central to database analysis.

So far, we have suppressed the names of the transitions. They really were not very interesting, and were certainly a distraction to our thread of thinking. We begin with two relations, the In and Out functions of the formal mathematical definition of a Petri net. Table 7.3 shows the In and Out database population for the composed Petri net in Figure 7.20.

If we wanted to, we could draw a Petri net very similar to that of Figure 7.20, based on the information in our database. The important thing is that we can understand Petri net composition as the continued population of our database. In fact, Table 7.3 also describes the Petri nets in Figures 7.21 and 7.22. We could compose the information in Figure 7.23 by first naming the unnamed transitions and then showing p14 as an input to each place. This database view of composition solves the diagramming and scale-up problems of Petri nets, but the connectivity is hidden. Clever database queries can produce connectivity information, but that is outside the scope of this book.

Rather than develop an overall Petri net that is more complex than the FSM in Figure 6.6, we will just note the size and density of connectivity. There are ten

Table 7.4 Transition Table for the Espresso Vending Machine

	e1: Insert €0.20 Coin	e2: Insert €0.50 Coin	e2: Insert €1.00 Coin	e4: Request Coin Return
p1: total is €0.00	p2	p7	p6	...
p2: total is €0.20	p3	p8	p10	p1
p3: total is €0.40	p4	p9	p10	p1
p4: total is €0.60	p5	p6	p10	p1
p5: total is €0.80	p6	p10	p10	p1
p6: total is €1.00	p10	p10	p10	p1
p7: total is €0.50	p8	p10	p10	p1
p8: total is €0.70	p9	p10	p10	p1
p9: total is €0.90	p10	p10	p10	p1
p10: total > €1.00	...	...	...	p1

states, four input events that can occur in most states, and two output events that occur on transitions to the p6 (€1.00) state. From Table 7.4, we calculate that the overall Petri net will have 36 individual transitions. At this point, the database approach is clearly preferable.

7.3.4 Smart Fuel Pump

The size and internal connectivity of the Smart Fuel Pump problem almost demand a bottom-up approach. Most of the elements of the problem are shown in Figure 7.24. The input events, output actions (also events), and states used in the figure are listed in Table 7.5.

The transitions are almost in a "natural order"; certainly the subnets are. In several places, we see that an input place of one subnet is an output of a "previous" subnet. The transaction-approval subnet, for example, when it executes, leaves a token in place p2 (pump enabled). This place is a precondition for the fuel-grade-selection subnet, and it, in turn, leaves place p5 marked, which is a precondition for the gun remove/replace subnet. The end-transaction subnet shows the two main ways to finish a full transaction: either by the fuel level dropping below the 4% level or by customer choice.

There are some subtle problems with the (nearly) full Petri net in Figure 7.25. All of the input events (labeled e1, e2, ...) have a zero indegree. How then can we

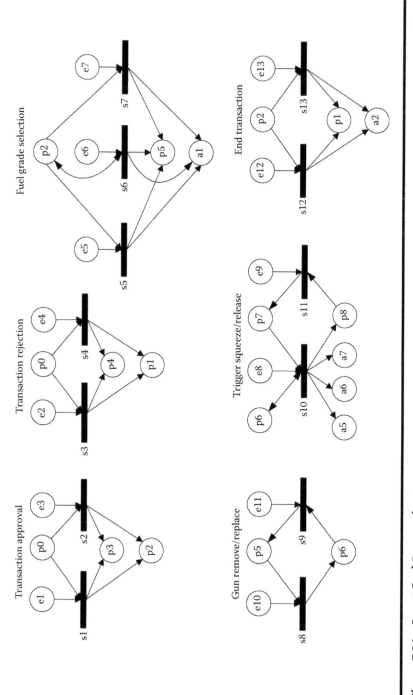

Figure 7.24 Smart Fuel Pump subnets.

Table 7.5 Smart Fuel Pump Events and States

Input Events	Output Events	States
e1: attendant approve	a1: start pump motor	p0: idle
e2: attendant reject	a2: stop pump motor	p1: pump disabled
e3: credit card approve	a3: engage pump clutch	p2: pump enabled
e4: credit card reject	a4: reset displays	p3: transaction approved
e5: select regular grade	a5: free pump clutch	p4: transaction rejected
e6: select mid-grade	a6: update volume pumped display	p5: fuel grade selected
e7: select premium grade	a7: update transaction-cost display	p6: gun replaced
e8: squeeze trigger	...	p7: gun removed
e9: release trigger	...	p8: trigger released
e10: remove gun	...	...
e11: replace gun	...	...
e12: tank level below 4%	...	...
e13: customer ends fuel delivery	...	...

ever execute this net? Once we have an initial marking, we could just mark every input event, but this might not be what we really intend. We shall see in Chapter 8 that event-driven Petri nets (EDPNs) solve this problem.

7.3.5 Saturn Windshield Wiper Controller

Table 7.6 defines the input events, output events, and states for the Saturn Windshield Wiper Controller Petri net. The actual net is shown in Figure 7.26. Notice that the subnet composed of transitions s1, s2, s3, s4, s5, and s6 corresponds to the Lever finite state machine we saw in Chapter 6 (Figure 6.10). Similarly, the subnet composed of transitions s7, s8, s9, and s10 corresponds to the Dial finite state machine. The subnet composed of transitions s11, s12, and s13 shows how the

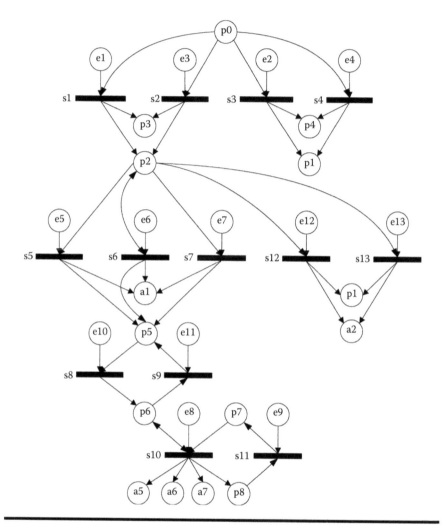

Figure 7.25   Smart Fuel Pump Petri net.

Table 7.6   Saturn Windshield Wiper Controller Events and States

Input Events	Output Events	States
e1: move lever up one position	a1: deliver 0 wipes per minute	p1: lever at OFF
e2: move lever down one position	a2: deliver 6 wipes per minute	p2: lever at INT
e3: move dial up one position	a3: deliver 12 wipes per minute	p3: lever at LOW

Table 7.6 Saturn Windshield Wiper Controller Events and States (Continued)

Input Events	Output Events	States
e4: move dial down one position	a4: deliver 20 wipes per minute	p4: lever at HIGH
...	a5: deliver 30 wipes per minute	p5: dial at 1
...	a6: deliver 60 wipes per minute	p6: dial at 2
...	...	p7: dial at 3

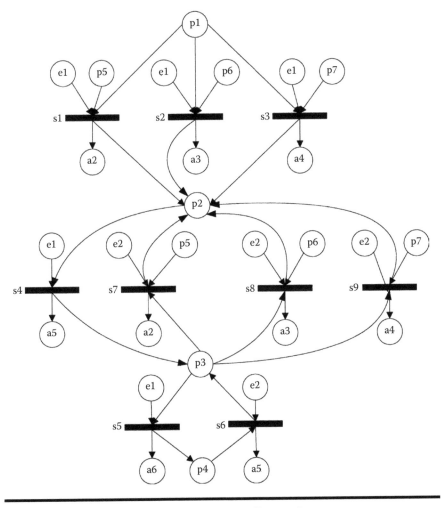

Figure 7.26   Saturn Windshield Wiper Controller Petri net.

individual finite state machines communicate, thereby avoiding the complexity of a Cartesian product finite state machine, as in Figure 6.11.

7.4 Petri Net Engines

Petri net engines are similar to finite state machine engines, at least at the interactive level. Given a Petri net, its possible execution tables indicate how a Petri net engine will execute a Petri net. (See Table 7.1 for a short execution table for the Producer–Consumer problem.)

A Petri net engine needs a definition of all places, the input and output functions relating places to transitions, and an initial marking, similar to the one in Table 7.1. Then the engine (and the user) proceed as follows:

1. The engine determines a list of all enabled transitions.
2.1 If no transition is enabled, the net is deadlocked.
2.2 If only one transition is enabled, it is automatically fired, and a new marking is generated.
2.3 If more than one transition is enabled, the user must select one to fire, and then a new marking is generated. (Note that the user resolves any Petri net conflict.)
3. The engine returns to step 1 and repeats until either the user stops or the net is deadlocked.

There are seven levels of Petri net execution. Incidentally, they correspond exactly to execution levels for statecharts.

Level 1 (Interactive): The user provides an initial marking, then directs transition firing, as described above.

Level 2 (Burst Mode): If there is a chain of steps in which only one transition is enabled, the whole chain is fired.

Level 3 (Predetermined): An input script marks places and directs execution.

Level 4 (Batch Mode): A set of predetermined scripts is executed.

Level 5 (Probabilistic): Similar to the interactive mode, only conflicts are resolved using transition-firing probabilities (e.g., at step 2.3).

Level 6 (Traffic Mix): A demographic set of batch scripts, executed in random order.

Level 7 (Exhaustive): For a system with no loops, execute all possible "threads." Exhaustive execution is more sensibly done with respect to the reachability tree of a Petri net. If a system has loops, the use of condensation graphs can produce a loop-free version. This is computationally intense, as a given initial marking may generate many possible threads, and the process should be repeated for many initial markings.

7.5 Advantages and Limitations

Petri nets are much more popular in Europe than in the United States. They are extremely expressive, and they finally help us understand some of the nuances of the behavioral issues (see Table 7.7) introduced in Chapter 3. Another advantage

Table 7.7   Representation of Behavioral Issues with Petri Nets

Issue	Represented?	Comments/Example
Sequence	yes	Figure 7.6
Selection	yes	Figure 7.7 (awkward)
Repetition	yes	Figure 7.6
Enable	yes	Figure 7.8
Disable	yes	Figure 7.8
Trigger	yes	Figure 7.9
Activate	yes	Figure 7.8
Suspend	yes	Figure 7.10
Resume	yes	Figure 7.10
Pause	yes	Figure 7.10
Conflict	yes	Figure 7.11
Priority	yes	Figure 7.12
Mutual exclusion	yes	Figure 7.13
Concurrent execution	yes	Figure 7.14
Deadlock	yes	Observed in a marking sequence
Context-sensitive input events	indirectly	Coin insertion in the Espresso Vending Machine
Multiple-context output events	indirectly	Transitions to €1.00 in the Espresso Vending Machine
Asynchronous events	indirectly	Depends on marking sequence
Event quiescence	indirectly	Depends on marking sequence

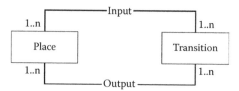

Figure 7.27   E/R model of a Petri net database.

is that they constitute a bottom-up approach (appropriate for agile development), and can easily be composed into larger nets. As just noted, Petri net engines provide extensive analytic capabilities very early in a project, so they support the executability goal described in Chapter 1. Finally, they allow the recognition and analysis of situations such as starvation (conflict in which one transition always fires), deadlock, and mutual exclusion. Petri nets are probably best used for an extremely "close look" at important portions of a system.

The biggest problem with Petri nets is that the graphical version does not scale up well. This can be mitigated by using a database with relations for the information in a Petri net, and then developing sets of useful queries. An E/R (entity/relation) model of such a database is given in Figure 7.27. The database possibility completely resolves the scale-up problem, but the resolution is at the expense of visual clarity. Closely related to this, most users find that they use a key (or legend) to give short names to Petri net places and transitions, thereby impairing communication.

Also, they do not deal with selection in a convenient way: Outcomes of a decision must be input places to two transitions that are in conflict. Another disadvantage (resolved by event-driven Petri nets) is that they do not represent event-driven systems well. In an execution table, or with an engine, there is no way to mark a place that corresponds to an input event. Also, once places that correspond to output events are marked, they remain marked. Finally, Petri nets are dismal at describing mathematical calculations. Technically, Petri nets do not represent concurrency, as only one transition can be fired at a time. This can be circumvented by assigning subnets to separate devices. This deficiency will be elegantly resolved with statecharts.

References

Bruyn, W., R. Jensen, D. Keskar, and P. Ward. 1988. ESML: An extended systems modeling language based on the data flow diagram. *ACM Software Engineering Notes* 13 (1): 58–67.

Exercises

1. Express the Windchill Factor Table problem as a Petri net. Discuss how well the problem is represented.
2. Express the Previous Date problem as a Petri net. Discuss how well the problem is represented.
3. Express the Saturn Cruise Control problem as a Petri net. Discuss how well the problem is represented.
4. Express the Programmable Thermostat problem as a Petri net. Discuss how well the problem is represented.
5. Express the Railroad Crossing Gate Controller problem as a Petri net. Discuss how well the problem is represented.
6. Express the Six-Coin Espresso Vending Machine (see Chapter 3) as a Petri net. Compare your Petri net to the one in the text. Does the simplification make the Petri net model any more useful?
7. Try following the 13 rules of the final NextDate decision table (Table 5.19) in the Petri net in Figure 7.17.
8. Develop a series of Petri nets for the €0.50-coin in the Espresso Vending Machine problem.
9. Finite state machines are a special case of Petri nets. Characterize the Petri net that corresponds to a given FSM. Hint: Note the indegree and outdegree of Petri net transitions.
10. Make an execution table for the Petri net in Figure 7.26. Use an initial marking of <1, 0, 0, 0, 1, 0, 0> and the event sequence <e1, e3, e1, e3, e1, e2, e4, e3>. Be sure to note the output events as they occur.

Chapter 8

Event-Driven Petri Nets

Basic Petri nets need two slight enhancements to become event-driven Petri nets (EDPNs). The first enables them to express more closely event-driven systems, and the second deals with Petri net markings that express event quiescence, an important notion in object-oriented applications. Taken together, these extensions result in an effective, operational modeling view of software requirements.

8.1 Definition and Notation

Definition

An *event-driven Petri net* is a tripartite-directed graph (P, D, S, In, Out) composed of three sets of nodes (P, D, S) and two mappings (In, Out), where

> P is a set of port events
> D is a set of data places
> S is a set of transitions
> In is a set of ordered pairs from $(P \cup D) \times S$
> Out is a set of ordered pairs from $S \times (P \cup D)$

EDPNs express four of the five basic system constructs defined in Chapter 1; only devices are missing. The set S of transitions corresponds to ordinary Petri net transitions, which are interpreted as actions. There are two kinds of places, port events and data places, and these are inputs to or outputs of transitions in S as defined by the input and output functions In and Out. The graphical symbols for EDPNs are shown in Figure 8.1

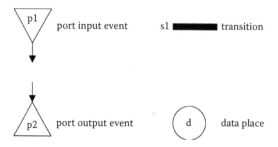

Figure 8.1   Graphical symbols for event-driven Petri nets.

Definition

A *thread* is a sequence of transitions in an event-driven Petri net.

We can always construct the inputs and outputs of a thread from the inputs and outputs of the transitions in the thread. EDPNs are graphically represented in much the same way as ordinary Petri nets; the only difference is the use of triangles for port-event places. In the EDPN in Figure 8.2 there are four transitions, s1, s2, s3, and s4, two port input events, p1 and p2, two port output

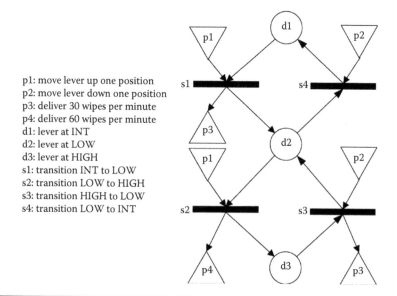

p1: move lever up one position
p2: move lever down one position
p3: deliver 30 wipes per minute
p4: deliver 60 wipes per minute
d1: lever at INT
d2: lever at LOW
d3: lever at HIGH
s1: transition INT to LOW
s2: transition LOW to HIGH
s3: transition HIGH to LOW
s4: transition LOW to INT

Figure 8.2   EDPN for part of the Saturn Windshield Wiper.

events, p3 and p4, and four data places, d1, d2, d3, and d4. This is the EDPN that corresponds to a portion of the finite state machine developed for the Saturn Windshield Wiper Controller.

8.1.1 Transition Enabling and Firing

Markings for an EDPN are more complicated because we want to be able to deal with event quiescence.

Definition

A *marking M of an EDPN* (P, D, S, In, Out) is a sequence M = <m1, m2,...> of p-tuples, where p = k + n, and k and n are the number of elements in the sets P and D, respectively. Individual entries in a p-tuple indicate the number of tokens in the event or data place.

Token movement and creation in an EDPN require closer attention. There are only two ways a data place can be marked: either by an initial marking or by firing a transition. The only way an output event can be marked is by firing a transition. Other than an initial marking, the only way to mark an input event is by choices made by the person who is executing the EDPN. This captures the event-driven nature of event-driven systems exactly.

Token duration also requires a more detailed view. Tokens in data places are as they were in ordinary Petri nets. Tokens in events are different, partly because events can be either discrete or continuous.

Definition

A *discrete event*, either input or output, is one that has a very short, and possibly an instantaneous, duration.

In the Saturn Windshield Wiper Controller, lever moves and dial moves are discrete events.

Definition

A *continuous event*, either input or output, is one that has a measurable duration.

In the Saturn Windshield Wiper Controller, the output events that deliver wiper strokes are nicely thought of as continuous events.

How long does a continuous output event remain marked? This is very dependent on the application, but there is one clear case: when a continuous output event

Table 8.1   A Marking of the EDPN in Figure 8.2

Time Step	<p1, p2, d1, d2, d3, p3, p4>	Description
m0	<0, 0, 1, 0, 0, 0, 0>	initial condition, in state d1
m1	<1, 0, 1, 0, 0, 0, 0>	event p1 occurs, s1 is enabled
m2	<0, 0, 0, 1, 0, 1, 0>	result of s1 firing, p3 occurs
m3	<1, 0, 0, 1, 0, 0, 0>	event p1 occurs, s2 is enabled
m4	<0, 0, 0, 0, 1, 0, 1>	result of s2 firing, p4 occurs
m5	<0, 1, 0, 0, 1, 0, 0>	event p2 occurs, s3 is enabled
m6	<0, 0, 0, 1, 0, 1, 0>	result of s3 firing, p3 occurs
m7	<0, 1, 0, 1, 0, 0, 0>	event p2 occurs, s4 is enabled
m8	<0, 0, 1, 0, 0, 0, 0>	result of s4 firing, no output event

occurs as a result of a transition firing that leaves the net in event quiescence. Then, we can think of the duration of the continuous output event as the duration of the event quiescent interval. In the Saturn Windshield Wiper Controller, the output events all occur at points of event quiescence, so, for example, if the lever is in the Low position, we can think of the output event p3 (deliver 30 w.p.s.) as continuously operating until some lever input event ends the event quiescence.

By convention, we will put the input event places first, followed by the data places, and then the output event places. An EDPN may have any number of markings, each corresponding to an execution of the net. Table 8.1 shows a sample marking of the EDPN in Figure 8.2.

The rules for transition enabling and firing in an EDPN are exact analogs of those for traditional Petri nets; a transition is enabled if there is at least one token in each input place, and when an enabled transition fires, one token is removed from each of its input places, and one token is placed in each of its output places. The "Time Step" column in Table 8.1 needs some explanation. Recall our refined definition of states in a finite state machine: an interval of time in which a certain proposition is true. The same definition applies to data places in an EDPN when they refer to states or conditions.

Definition

A transition in an event-driven Petri net is *enabled* if there is at least one token in each of its input places.

Definition

When an enabled event-driven Petri net transition *fires*, one token is removed from each of its input places, and one token is added to each of its output places.

One important difference between EDPNs and traditional Petri nets is that event quiescence can be broken by creating a token in a port input event place. In traditional Petri nets, when no transition is enabled, we say that the net is dead-locked. In EDPNs, when no transition is enabled, the net is at a point of event quiescence. (Of course, if no event occurs, this is the same as deadlock.) Event quiescence occurs five times in the thread in Table 8.1: at steps m0, m2, m4, m6, and m8.

The individual members in a marking can be thought of as snapshots of the executing EDPN at discrete points in time. These members are alternatively referred to as time steps, p-tuples, or marking vectors. This lets us think of time as an ordering that allows us to recognize "before" and "after." If we attach instantaneous time as an attribute of port events, data places, and transitions, we obtain a much clearer picture of thread behavior. One awkward part to this is how to treat tokens in a port output event place. Port output places always have outdegree = 0; in an ordinary Petri net, there is no way for tokens to be removed from a place with a zero outdegree. If the tokens in a port output event place persist, this suggests that the event occurs indefinitely. Here again, the time attributes resolve the confusion; this time we need a duration of the marked output event. (Another possibility is to remove tokens from a marked output event place after one time step; this works reasonably well, as in Table 8.1.)

8.2 Technique

Here are some general hints for using event-driven Petri nets:

1. Use transitions to represent actions.
2. Use data places to represent any of the following:
   - Data
   - Pre- and postconditions
   - States
   - Messages
3. Use events to represent
   - Port input events
   - Port output events
   - Passage of time
4. Use the Input relationship to represent prerequisites and inputs.
5. Use the Output relationship to represent consequences and outputs.
6. Use markings to represent "states" of a net, memory, or counters.

7. Tasks can be considered to be individual transitions or subnets.
8. Subsets of input data places to a transition can be used to define a context.

Because ordinary Petri nets are a special case of event-driven Petri nets, many of the behavioral issues described in Chapter 7 are identical in the event-driven Petri net form. The following issues therefore need no special description:

■ Sequence, selection, and repetition
■ Enable, disable, and activate
■ Trigger
■ Suspend, resume, and pause
■ Conflict and priority
■ Mutual exclusion
■ Synchronization

8.2.1 Context-Sensitive Input Events

The event e in Figure 8.3 is a context-sensitive input event to transitions s1 and s2. Notice that s1 and s2 are in Petri net conflict with respect to event e. Whichever context is marked determines the "meaning" of e. In good practice, the contexts of context-sensitive input events should be mutually exclusive. Similarly, the event o is an output event that occurs in multiple contexts.

8.2.2 Multiple-Context Output Events

The output event in Figure 8.3 can be caused either by s3 or by s4. With no history, once event o occurs, its cause is not known. This characterizes many field trouble reports where an unexpected output occurs, and its normal cause is not the reason.

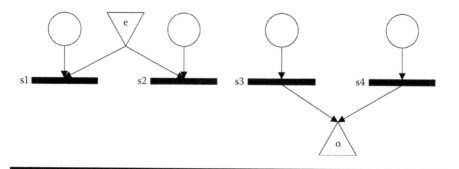

Figure 8.3 Context-sensitive input events and multiple-context output events.

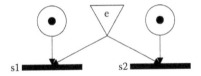

Figure 8.4 Event quiescence.

8.2.3 Event Quiescence

Transitions s1 and s2 in Figure 8.4 are disabled until event e occurs. If e never occurs, this would be deadlock. This is the event quiescence of event-driven systems, where nothing happens until an event occurs.

8.3 Examples

The variable names and other notation used in these figures are taken from those defined in Chapter 3.

8.3.1 Simplified U.S. 1040EZ Income Tax Form

There are no events in the Simplified U.S. 1040EZ Income Tax Form, so an event-driven Petri net formulation is identical to the ordinary Petri net formulation in Figure 7.16. Just as the ordinary Petri net formulation is unnecessarily complex, the event-driven Petri net formulation would be worse. We could probably postulate input events for entry of the input data values, but that is stretching the notation.

8.3.2 The NextDate Function

As with the Simplified U.S. 1040EZ Income Tax Form, an event-driven Petri net formulation is identical to the ordinary Petri net formulation in Figure 7.17. Just as the ordinary Petri net formulation is unnecessarily complex, the event-driven Petri net formulation would be worse.

8.3.3 Espresso Vending Machine

The Espresso Vending Machine is clearly an event-driven system, so EDPNs will be a good choice. Figure 8.5 is the EDPN equivalent of the ordinary Petri net formulation in Figure 7.19. The minor changes:

- Ordinary Petri net places are renamed as EDPN data places
- Ordinary Petri net places that represented events are renamed and drawn as triangles

d1: total is € 0.00
d2: total is € 0.20
d3: total is € 0.40
d4: total is € 0.60
d5: total is € 0.80
d6: total is € 1.00
d7: total is € 0.50
d8: total is € 0.70
d9: total is € 0.90
d10: total is € 1.10
p1: insert € 0.20 coin
p2: insert € 0.50 coin
p3: insert € 1.00 coin
p4: request coin return
p5: dispense espresso
p6: return coins

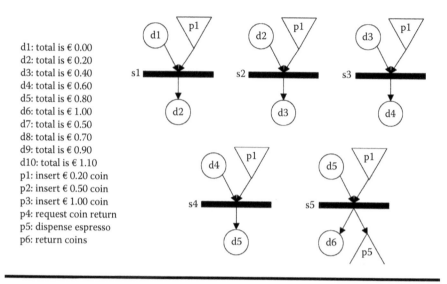

Figure 8.5   A few EDPNs for the Espresso Vending Machine.

Event-driven Petri nets can be composed in much the same way as ordinary Petri nets, but it makes no sense to connect an output event to anything other than a transition. Figure 8.6 shows one possible composition of the subnets in Figure 8.5.

The composition in Figure 8.6 captures the sequence of the €0.20-coin insertion events to total €1.00. It also shows that event p1 is context sensitive: In some contexts

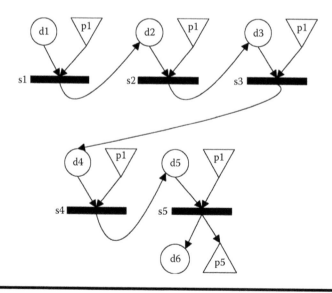

Figure 8.6   One composition of the subnets in Figure 8.5.

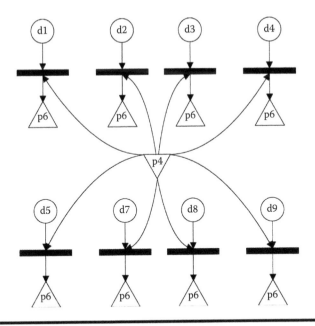

Figure 8.7   Composition with respect to event p4.

there is no observable output event, but in the €1.00 context, it produces the output event p5. We could go through the motions of different compositions, as we did in Figures 7.21 and 7.22, but both of those suppress the sequence of five coin insertions. Sometimes, composition with respect to an input (or output) event is helpful, as in Figure 8.7. There, event p4 can occur in any context in which the total is less than €1.00. In each context, the output event p6 (return all coins) occurs. Note that event p4 is not a context-sensitive input event; the output is always the same, event p6. Would it have been helpful to also compose with respect to event p6? Not really. It is an event that occurs in multiple contexts, and this is clearly shown.

The rest of the Espresso Vending Machine requires EDPNs similar to those in Figures 8.5, 8.6, and 8.7 for the €0.50- and €1.00-coin insertion events. As we did with ordinary Petri nets, this is the point at which it is better to switch to table-based definitions. The scale-up limits of EDPNs are painfully clear here. Once again, we can view EDPN composition as the population of a database. The E/R (Entity Relationship) Model in Figure 8.8 contains all the relations needed to fully describe an EDPN. All relations are many-to-many with optional participation, i.e., their UML (Unified Modeling Language) min/max descriptions are all (0..n).

8.3.4 Smart Fuel Pump

The Smart Fuel Pump problem has several context-sensitive input events. The list of events and states from Table 7.5 is revised here to EDPN terms in Figure 8.9.

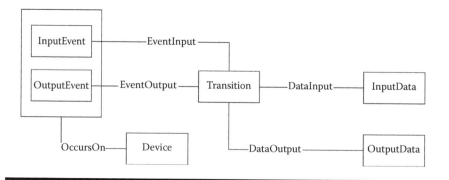

Figure 8.8. E/R model of an EDPN database.

p1: attendant approve
p2: attendant reject
p3: credit card approve
p4: credit card reject
p5: select regular grade
p6: select mid-grade
p7: select premium grade
p8: squeeze trigger
p9: release trigger
p10: remove gun
p11: replace gun
p12: tank level below 4%
p13: customer ends fuel delivery

p21: start pump motor
p22: stop pump motor
p23: engage pump clutch
p24: reset displays
p25: free pump clutch
p26: update volume pumped display
p27: update transaction cost display

d1: pump disabled
d2: pump enabled
d3: transaction approved
d4: transaction rejected
d5: fuel grade selected
d6: gun replaced
d7: gun removed
d8: trigger released

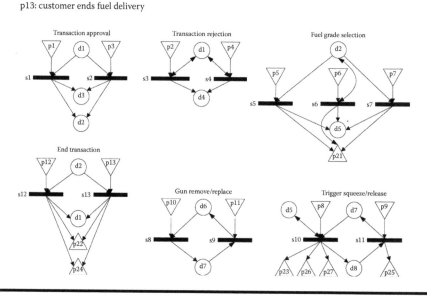

Figure 8.9. Smart Fuel Pump EDPNs.

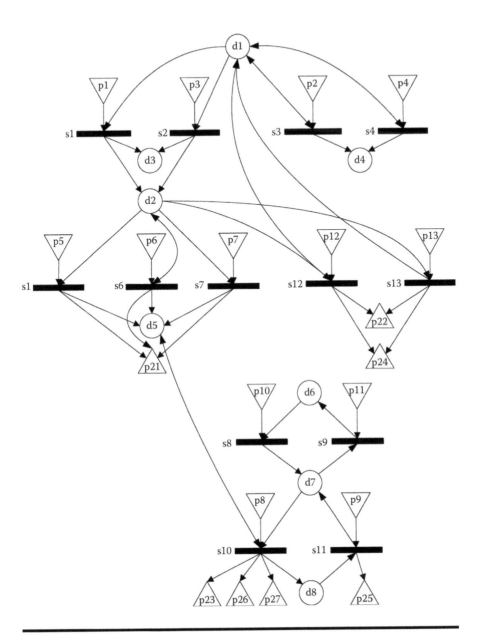

Figure 8.10. Smart Fuel Pump EDPN.

The full EDPN from composing the individual EDPNs in Figure 8.9 is shown in Figure 8.10. Why bother? If you look carefully at Figure 8.10, you might notice that place d6 (gun replaced) is an interesting input. The only way it can be marked is by firing transition s9, which is fired when p11 (replace gun) is fired. Most of the full EDPN refers to a single transaction, but gun replacement had to occur in a (the!) previous transaction. This level of detail cannot be seen in the individual EDPNs as in Figure 8.9. Another detailed question relates to d3 (transaction approved) and d4 (transaction rejected). Once either place is marked, there is no way to unmark it. Presumably, this would occur by an action (event!) performed by either the attendant or the credit card company.

8.3.5 Saturn Windshield Wiper Controller

The EDPN for the full Saturn Windshield Wiper Controller is shown in Figure 8.11. The input edges from places d2 (lever at Int) and from places d5, d6, and d7 (dial positions) are all double-headed connections. Otherwise, transitions s11, s12, and s13 could only fire once. Table 8.2 is an execution table for a sample scenario. When an EDPN has many places, it is simpler to just indicate the marked places, as in Table 8.2.

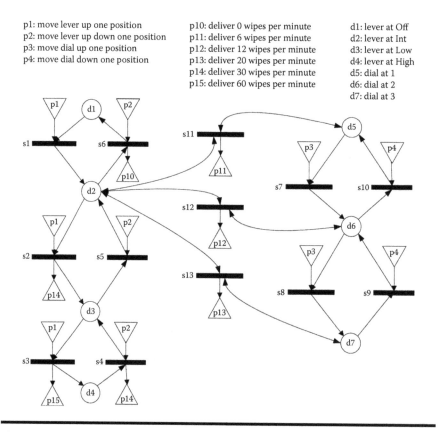

p1: move lever up one position
p2: move lever up down one position
p3: move dial up one position
p4: move dial down one position

p10: deliver 0 wipes per minute
p11: deliver 6 wipes per minute
p12: deliver 12 wipes per minute
p13: deliver 20 wipes per minute
p14: deliver 30 wipes per minute
p15: deliver 60 wipes per minute

d1: lever at Off
d2: lever at Int
d3: lever at Low
d4: lever at High
d5: dial at 1
d6: dial at 2
d7: dial at 3

Figure 8.11   Saturn Windshield Wiper Controller EDPN.

Table 8.2   EDPN Execution Table for the Saturn Windshield Wiper Controller

Time Step	Fired Transition	Input Event	Marked Input Events and Places	Enabled Transitions	Output Event	Marked Output Events and Places	Event Quiescent?
m0	...	...	d1, d5	(none)	...	...	yes
m1	...	p1	p1, d1, d5	s1	...	...	no
m2	s1	...	d2, d5	s11	...	d2, d5	no
m3	s11	...	d2, d5	s11*	p11	d2, d5, p11	(yes)
m4	...	p3	p3, d2, d5	s7, s11*	...	d2,d5	no
m5	s7	...	d2, d6	s12	...	...	no
m6	s12	...	d2, d6	s12*	p12	d2, d6, p12	(yes)
m7	...	p1	p1, d2, d6	s2, s12*	...	...	no
m8	s2	...	d3, d6	...	p14	d3, d6, p14	yes
m9	...	p1	p1, d3, d6	s3	...	d3, d6	no
m10	s3	...	d4, d6	...	p15	d4, d6, p14	yes
m11	...	p2	p2, d4, d6	s4	...	d4, d6	no
m12	s4	...	d3, d6	...	p14	d3, d6, p14	yes
m13	...	p3	p3, d3, d6	s8	...	d3, d6	no
m14	s8	...	d3, d7	...	...	d3, d7	yes
m15	...	p2	p2, d3, d7	s5	...	d3, d7	no
m16	s5	...	d2, d7	s13	...	d2, d7	no
m17	s13	...	d2, d7	s13*	p13	d2, d7	(yes)
m18	...	p2	p2, d2, d7	s6, s13*	...	d2, d7	no
m19	s6	...	d1, d7	...	p10	d1, d7	yes

* Enabled transitions s11, s12, and s13 are problematic. If we consider events p11, p12, and p13 to be continuous output events, we only want to fire these transitions once. If we consider them to be instantaneous events, we would need to add a timeout event and some kind of interlock with the lever transitions.

Table 8.3 Representation of Behavioral Issues with EDPNs

Behavioral Issue	Represented in EDPNs?
Sequence	yes
Selection	yes, but awkward
Repetition	yes
Enable	yes
Disable	yes
Trigger	yes
Activate	yes
Suspend	yes
Resume	yes
Pause	yes
Priority	yes
Mutual exclusion	yes
Concurrent execution	yes, but need devices
Deadlock	yes
Context-sensitive input events	yes
Multiple-context output events	yes
Asynchronous events	yes
Event quiescence	yes

Executing an EDPN is more complex than executing an ordinary Petri net because there are two distinct types of events: discrete and continuous. These relate to marking, the duration of a time step, and event quiescence. Events p1, p2, p3, and p4 are all discrete events, in the sense that they occur instantaneously. The output events (p10–p15) are best understood as continuous, in the sense that they deliver various wiper speeds for the duration of the time step in which they occur.

Table 8.2 shows an execution table that could be produced by an EDPN engine. It follows the use case introduced in Chapter 6.

In time step m1, since p1 occurs, we cannot say that the system is event quiescent. But, since p1 is a discrete event (with instantaneous duration), transition s1 is enabled. If we decide that, when only one transition in an EDPN is enabled, it fires immediately, then all of time step m1 is instantaneous. Otherwise, we can show the transition firing as a separate step, and in step m2.

In time step m3 (similarly for m6 and m17), since p11 occurs, no transition is enabled. So now we must clarify what we mean by event quiescence.

> Choice 1: no transition is enabled, waiting for an input event
> Choice 2: no transition is enabled, a continuous output event is occurring
> Choice 3: the EDPN is truly deadlocked, i.e., there is no input event that can enable a transition

In step m4, transitions s7 and s11 are in conflict. The EDPN is quiescent until the conflict is resolved, but how might this happen? If a customer executes the model, using an EDPN engine, the customer choice is, in a curious sense, also an input.

8.4 Event-Driven Petri Net Engines

Because event-driven Petri nets are an extension of ordinary Petri nets, there are only a few differences between their respective engines. Given an event-driven Petri net, its possible execution tables indicate how its engine will operate. (See Table 8.2 for a short execution table for the Saturn Windshield Wiper problem.)

An EDPN engine needs a definition of all input events, output events, places, the input and output functions relating these to transitions, and an initial marking, similar to the one in Table 8.2. Then the engine (and the user) proceed as follows:

1. The engine determines a list of all enabled transitions.
2.1 If no transition is enabled, the net is either at a point of event quiescence or it is deadlocked.
2.2 If an input event can break event quiescence, the user causes (symbolically) an input event to occur. If more than one input event can end event quiescence, the user chooses which event to cause.
2.3 If the EDPN is deadlocked, the engine ends execution.
3.1 If only one transition is enabled, it is automatically fired, and a new marking is generated.
3.2 If more than one transition is enabled, the user must select one to fire, and then a new marking is generated. (Note that the user resolves any Petri net conflict.)
3.3 If transition firing causes an output event, that event is marked until the next execution step.
4. The engine returns to step 1 and repeats until either the user stops or the net is deadlocked.

There are seven levels of event-driven Petri net execution; they correspond exactly to execution levels for ordinary Petri nets (and statecharts).

Level 1 (Interactive): The user provides an initial marking, then directs transition firing, as described above.

Level 2 (Burst Mode): If there is a chain of steps in which only one transition is enabled, the whole chain is fired.

Level 3 (Predetermined): An input script marks places and directs execution.

Level 4 (Batch Mode): A set of predetermined scripts is executed.

Level 5 (Probabilistic): Similar to the interactive mode, only conflicts are resolved using transition firing probabilities (e.g., at step 2.3).

Level 6 (Traffic Mix): A demographic set of batch scripts, executed in random order.

Level 7 (Exhaustive): For a system with no loops, execute all possible "threads." Exhaustive execution is more sensibly done with respect to the reachability tree of a Petri net. If a system has loops, the use of condensation graphs can produce a loop-free version. This is computationally intense, as a given initial marking may generate many possible threads, and the process should be repeated for many initial markings.

8.5 Advantages and Limitations

Event-driven Petri nets inherit all of the advantages of ordinary Petri nets, but the addition of event places removes a few limitations. The primary advantage of EDPNs is their explicit modeling of events. This, in turn, permits the recognition of event-related issues such as event quiescence, context-sensitive input events, and multiple-context output events. Like ordinary Petri nets, they constitute a bottom-up approach (appropriate for agile development), and can easily be composed into larger nets. As just noted, EDPN engines provide extensive analytic capabilities very early in a project, so they support the executability goal described in Chapter 1. Finally, they allow the recognition and analysis of situations such as starvation (conflict in which one transition always fires), deadlock, and mutual exclusion. Petri nets are probably best used for an extremely "close look" at important portions of a system.

The biggest problem with Petri nets is that the graphical version does not scale up well. This can be mitigated by using a database with relations for the information in an event-driven Petri net, and then developing sets of useful queries. An E/R model of such a database is given in Figure 8.8. The database possibility completely resolves the scale-up problem, but the resolution is at the expense of visual clarity. Closely related to this, most users find that they use a key (or legend) to give short names to Petri net places and transitions, thereby impairing communication.

Also, Petri nets do not deal with selection in a convenient way: Outcomes of a decision must be input places to two transitions that are in conflict. Another disadvantage (resolved by event-driven Petri nets) is that they do not represent event-driven systems well. In an execution table, or with an engine, there is no way to mark a place that corresponds to an input event. Also, once places that correspond to output events are marked, they remain marked. Finally, Petri nets are dismal at describing mathematical calculations. Technically, event-driven Petri nets do not represent concurrency, as only one transition can be fired at a time. However, as with ordinary Petri nets, this can be circumvented by assigning subnets to separate devices. This deficiency will be elegantly resolved with statecharts.

Exercises

1. Express the Windchill Factor Table problem as an event-driven Petri net. Discuss how well the problem is represented.
2. Express the Previous Date problem as an event-driven Petri net. Discuss how well the problem is represented.
3. Express the Saturn Cruise Control problem as an event-driven Petri net. Discuss how well the problem is represented.
4. Express the Programmable Thermostat problem as an event-driven Petri net. Discuss how well the problem is represented.
5. Express the Railroad Crossing Gate Controller problem as an event-driven Petri net. Discuss how well the problem is represented.
6. Express the Six-Coin Espresso Vending Machine (see Chapter 3) as an event-driven Petri net. Compare your Petri net to the one in the text. Does the simplification make the event-driven Petri net model any more useful?
7. Complete the "Event Quiescent?" column of Table 8.2 for time steps m10 to m14.
8. Make an EDPN execution table for the following scenario, defined by an initial marking and a sequence of input events:

   Initial marking: lever at Off, dial at position 2
   Event sequence: <p1, p1, p1, p3, p2, p2, p4, p4, p2>

Chapter 9

Statecharts

David Harel had two goals when he developed the statechart notation: He wanted to devise a visual notation that combined the ability of Venn diagrams to express hierarchy and the ability of directed graphs to express connectedness (Harel 1988). Taken together, these capabilities provide an elegant answer to the "state explosion" problem of ordinary finite state machines. The result is a highly sophisticated and very precise notation that is supported by commercially available CASE (computer-aided software engineering) tools, notably the StateMate system from IBM (see section 9.4 for the acquisition history). Statecharts are now the control model of choice for the Unified Modeling Language (UML) from the Object Management Group. (See www.omg.org for more details.)

9.1 Definition and Notation

Harel uses the methodology-neutral term "blob" to describe the basic building block of a statechart. Blobs can contain other blobs, similar to the way that Venn diagrams show set containment. Blobs can also be connected to other blobs with edges in the same way that nodes in a directed graph are connected. In Figure 9.1, blob A contains two blobs, B and C, and they are connected by edges. Blob A is also connected to blob D by an edge.

As Harel intends, we can interpret blobs as states, and edges as transitions. The full StateMate system supports an elaborate language that defines how and when transitions occur. (Their training course ran for a full week, so this section is a highly simplified introduction.) Statecharts are executable, in a much more elaborate way than ordinary finite state machines. Executing a statechart requires a notion similar to that of Petri net markings.

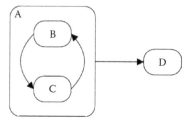

Figure 9.1   Blobs in a statechart.

There is one specialized difference between statechart blobs and the circles of a Venn diagram. In a Venn diagram, any point within a circle is assumed to be an element of the set represented by the circle. The same is not true for blob inclusion. In Figure 9.2, blob B is an element of blobs H and K (and also blob A). Similarly, blob D is an element of blobs G, H, and A, but there is nothing in the apparent intersection of blobs G and J. This distinction is enforced by the notion of contours, and contours are never allowed to coincide. Notice that blob B is dangerously close to the contour of blob H, but it is still distinct.

The "initial state" of a statechart is indicated by an edge that has no source state. When states are nested within other states, the same indication is used to show the lower-level initial state. In Figure 9.3, state A is the initial state, and when it is entered at the lower level, state B is also entered. When a state is entered, we can think of it as active, analogous to a marked place in a Petri net. (The StateMate tool uses colors to show which states are active, and this is equivalent to marking places in a Petri net.)

There is a subtlety in Figure 9.3: The transition from state A to state D seems ambiguous at first, because it has no apparent recognition of states B and C. The

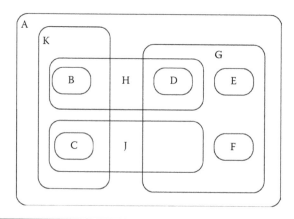

Figure 9.2   Convention of blob contours.

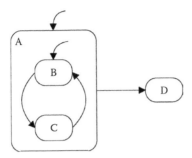

Figure 9.3   Initial states in a statechart.

convention is that edges must start and end on the contour of a state. Figure 9.4 demonstrates the reason for the "unique contour" convention: Since the contour of blob C coincides with the contour of blob A, there is no way to know the source state of the transition to state D.

If a state contains substates, as state A does, the edge "refers" to all substates. Thus the edge from A to D means that the transition can occur either from state B or from state C. If we had an edge from state D to state A, as in Figure 9.5, the

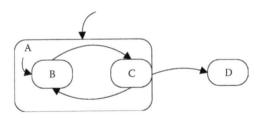

Figure 9.4   Ambiguous blob contours.

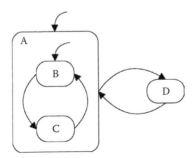

Figure 9.5   Default entry into substates.

fact that state B is indicated as the initial state means that the transition is really from state D to state B. This convention greatly reduces the tendency of finite state machines to look like "spaghetti code."

The statechart language is quite complex and represents a major extension to that of finite state machines. One basic idea is that statecharts now have memory (recall that finite state machines have no memory). This one change greatly enhances the expressive power of a statechart model.

Transitions are still caused by events and conditions (as described in Tables 9.1, 9.2, and 9.3).

The last aspect of statecharts that we will discuss is the notion of concurrent statecharts. In Figure 9.6, the dotted line in state D is used to show that state D really refers to two concurrent states, E and F. (Harel's convention is to move the state label of D to a rectangular tag on the contour of the state.) Although not

Table 9.1 Statechart Language Elements for Events

Event	Occurs when:
en(S)	State S is entered
ex(S)	State S is exited
entering(S)	State S is entered
exiting(S)	State S is exited
st(A)	Activity A is started
sp(A)	Activity A is stopped
ch(V)	The value of data item expression V is changed
tr(C)	The value of condition C is set to TRUE (from FALSE)
fs(C)	The value of condition C is set to FALSE (from TRUE)
rd(V)	Data item V is read
wr(V)	Data item V is written
tm(E,N)	N clock units passed from last time event E occurred
E(C)	E has occurred and condition C is TRUE
not E	E did not occur
E1 and E2	E1 and E2 occurred simultaneously
E1 or E2	E1 or E2, or both, occurred

Table 9.2 Statechart Language Elements for Conditions

Condition	TRUE when:
in(S)	System is in state S
ac(A)	Activity A is active
hg(A)	Activity A is suspended
EXP1 R EXP2	The value of the expression EXP1 and EXP2 satisfy the relation R. When expressions are numeric, R may be: =, /=, >, or <. When they are strings, R may be: = or /=
not C	C is not TRUE
C1 and C2	Both C1 and C2 are TRUE
C1 or C2	C1 or C2, or both, are TRUE

Table 9.3 Statechart Language Elements for Actions

Action	Performs:
E	Generate the event E
tr!(C)	Assign TRUE to the condition C
fs!(C)	Assign FALSE to the condition C
V:=EXP	Assign the value of EXP to the data item V
st!(A)	Activate the activity A
sp!(A)	Terminate the activity A
sd!(A)	Suspend the activity A
rs!(A)	Resume the activity A
rd!(V)	Read the value of data item V
wr!(V)	Write the value of data item V

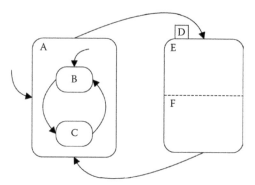

Figure 9.6   Concurrent states.

shown here, we can think of E and F as parallel machines (or better, devices) that execute concurrently. Because the edge from state A terminates on the contour of state D, when that transition occurs, both machines E and F are active (or marked, in the Petri net sense).

9.2 Technique

Figure 9.7 is taken directly from David Harel's seminal paper in 1988 (Harel 1988). He uses this example to describe statechart execution. It has three concurrent regions, labeled here as A, D, and H. On entry to the overall (not named) chart, the

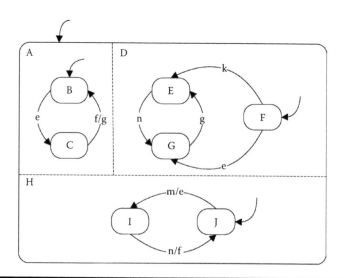

Figure 9.7   Broadcasting statechart from (Harel 1988).

Table 9.4   Execution Table for Harel's Broadcasting Example

Step	Active States	Input Event	Output Events	Next State(s)
0	B, F, J	k	(none)	E
1	B, E, J	m	e	I
2	B, E, I	e	(none)	C
3	C, E, I	n	f	G, J
4	C, G, J	f	g	B, G, J
5	B, G, J	g	(none)	B, E, J

initially active states are B, F, and J. We will follow an abstract scenario to see the effect of events on active states in Table 9.4.

9.3 Examples

The variable names and other notation used in these figures are taken from those defined in Chapter 3.

9.3.1 Simplified U.S. 1040EZ Income Tax Form

Harel's goal with the statechart notation was to reduce the "state explosion" common to finite state machines. He also designed the notation for reactive (event-driven) applications. The Simplified U.S. 1040EZ Income Tax Form is a strictly transforming application; there is no reaction to external events. As noted in Chapter 3, it belongs in the static sequential quadrant of the application domain. The only way to really use the expressive power of statecharts on this example is to assume that certain parts of the process could be conducted in parallel, as in Figure 9.8. The deductions and income portions of the form are independent, and can be done in either order, or they could be done in parallel (hardly likely, but this is an example!). Either way, both provide inputs to the tax computation blob. One defect remains: If either concurrent region finishes before the other, the tax computation will not have both inputs.

9.3.2 The NextDate Function

The NextDate function is another transformational application, completely data driven. About the only chance for anything interesting in a statechart is the possibility of parallel processing on the in-range checking of the input variables. We can show that in concurrent regions, as in Figure 9.9. The NextDate statechart is

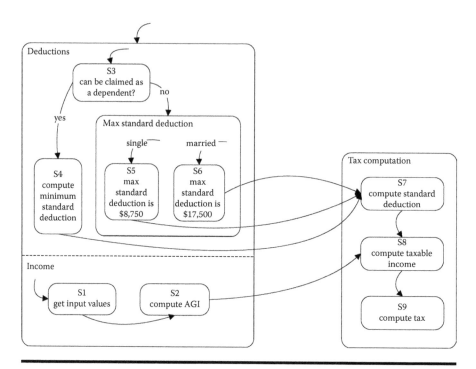

Figure 9.8   U.S. 1040EZ Form.

still rather "flowcharty" and it does not show the data dependencies as well as the decision table in Chapter 5, Tables 5.17 and 5.18.

9.3.3 Espresso Vending Machine

The events and actions in Figure 9.10 are exactly those used in Figures 6.4, 6.5, and 6.6. Here, we see the simplifying effect of a transition beginning at the contour of a state with interior states, for example the transition from the accepting-coins state to the coin-return state. The other good example is the transition from the accepting-coins state to the overpayment state caused by event e3 (insertion of a €1 coin).

We can clean up the four transitions caused by event e2 from the totals over €0.50 by creating two internal, compound states, as in Figure 9.11. Take a moment to compare Figures 9.10 and 9.11 with the traditional finite state machines in Figure 6.6. The horrible "spaghetti code" diagram is replaced by much cleaner ones, but this comes at a price. The information content in a statechart is significantly more dense, and this, in turn, makes statecharts more difficult as a subject of a

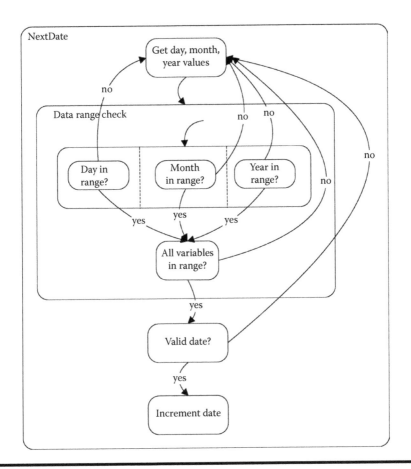

Figure 9.9 NextDate statechart.

technical inspection. The tool vendor's (correct) answer to this is that, rather than hold a technical inspection, it is preferable to let the customer execute the model, in much the same way that a customer uses a rapid prototype.

9.3.4 Smart Fuel Pump

We expand the smart fuel pump events slightly here (Figure 9.12). There are four interesting "devices" (which is a little dehumanizing for the attendant and the customer), and these devices perform the input events.

The customer can perform any of the events e1, e2, e7, e8, e9, e10, e11, e12, e13, and e15. The attendant can perform events e3 and e4. The credit card company can perform events e5 and e6. Finally, and perhaps most interestingly, the fuel tank can

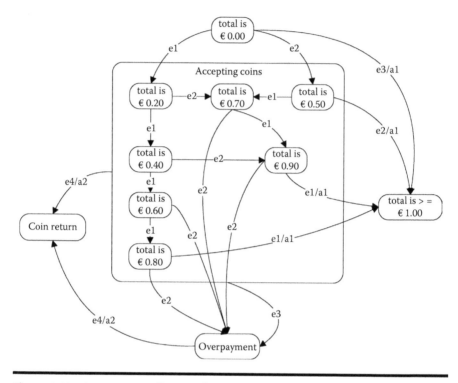

Figure 9.10   Espresso Vending Machine statechart.

perform event e14. Technically, the pump and the gun are also devices, but we will model them with the customer.

Smart Fuel Pump Events

e1: choose attendant pay
e2: choose credit card pay
e3: attendant approve
e4: attendant reject
e5: credit card approve
e6: credit card reject
e7: select regular grade
e8: select mid-grade

e9: select premium grade
e10: squeeze trigger
e11: release trigger
e12: remove gun
e13: replace gun
e14: tank level below 4%
e15: customer ends fuel delivery

Smart Fuel Pump Actions

a1: start pump motor
a2: stop pump motor
a3: engage pump clutch
a4: reset displays

a5: free pump clutch
a6: update volume pumped display
a7: update transaction cost display

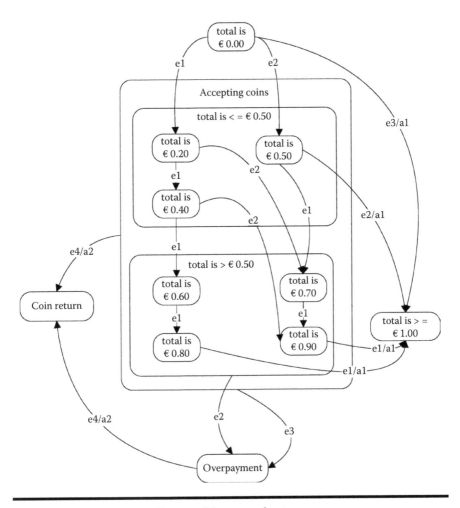

Figure 9.11   Espresso Vending Machine statechart.

9.3.5 *Saturn Windshield Wiper Controller*

Figure 9.13 is a statechart for the Saturn Windshield Wiper Controller.

e1: move lever up one position   e3: move dial up one position
e2: move lever down one position   e4: move dial down one position
a1: deliver 0 wipes per minute   a4: deliver 20 wipes per minute
a2: deliver 6 wipes per minute   a5: deliver 30 wipes per minute
a3: deliver 12 wipes per minute   a6: deliver 60 wipes per minute

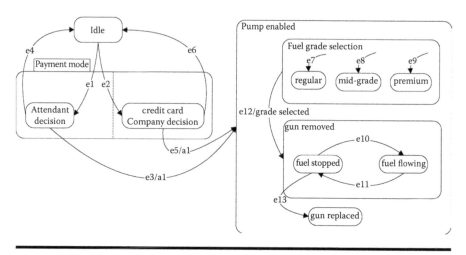

Figure 9.12 Smart Fuel Pump statechart.

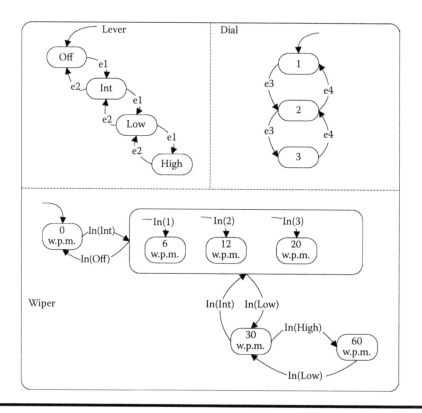

Figure 9.13 Saturn Windshield Wiper Controller statechart.

9.4 Statechart Engines

Recommending specific products is outside the scope of this book, so here is a description of the historical (circa 1990) StateMate system. (A Google search on "statechart engines" returned 141,000 hits!) The StateMate product from the i-Logix corporation (circa 1990) was the original, commercially available product that contained a statechart engine. This is not surprising, as David Harel was one of the founders of i-Logix. Since then, Telelogic acquired i-Logix in 2006, and in 2008, IBM acquired Telelogic.

Input to the original StateMate system is a statechart. There are seven levels of statechart execution. A statechart engine would produce an execution table similar to the one in Table 9.5, which traces the same use case scenario that was used in Chapters 6 and 8. Statechart execution has a notion of time steps, which are time intervals between input events. In Table 9.5, the first time step is split into three stages to show the effect of broadcasting. These stages are compressed into one in the remaining time steps. The statechart notation does not provide for direct expression of output events, but they are easily shown as states in a separate concurrent region. In the original StateMate system, outputs on transitions referred to actions that, in turn, generated output events.

Level 1 (Interactive): The user provides initial conditions, and then directs execution by providing input events.

Level 2 (Burst Mode): If there is a chain of steps in which only one transition is enabled, the whole chain is fired. If multiple transitions are enabled in separate concurrent regions, they all execute.

Level 3 (Predetermined): An input script marks places and directs execution.

Level 4 (Batch Mode): A set of predetermined scripts is executed.

Level 5 (Probabilistic): Similar to the interactive mode, only conflicts are resolved using transition firing probabilities (e.g., at step 2.3).

Level 6 (Traffic Mix): A demographic set of batch scripts, executed in random order.

Level 7 (Exhaustive): For a system with no loops, execute all possible "threads." Exhaustive execution is more sensibly done with respect to the reachability tree of a Petri net. If a system has loops, the use of condensation graphs can produce a loop-free version. This is computationally intense, as a given initial marking may generate many possible threads, and the process should be repeated for many initial markings.

9.5 Advantages and Limitations

Statecharts have two primary advantages: There are commercially available execution engines, and they scale up well to large, complex, concurrent applications. The main disadvantage is complexity, both of the notation and the language on

Table 9.5   Execution Table for the Saturn Windshield Wiper Controller

Step	Active States	Input Events	Next States	Output (Events)
1.1	Lever.Off, Dial.1, Wiper.0wpm	e1: move lever up one position	Lever.Int, Dial.1	In(Int), In(1)
1.2	Lever.Int, Dial.1	In(Int)	Lever.Int, Dial.1, Wiper.Int	...
1.3	...	In(1)	Lever.Int, Dial.1, Wiper. Int.6wpm	...
2	Lever.Int, Dial.1, Wiper. Int.6wpm	e3: move dial up one position	Lever.Int, Dial.2, Wiper. Int.12wpm	In(Int), In(2)
3	Lever.Int, Dial.2, Wiper. Int.12wpm	e1: move lever up one position	Lever.Low, Dial.2, Wiper.30wpm	In(Low), In(2)
4	Lever.Low, Dial.2, Wiper30wpm	e1: move lever up one position	Lever.High, Dial.2, Wiper.60wpm	In(High), In(2)
5	Lever.High, Dial.2, Wiper.60wpm	e2: move lever down one position	Lever.Low, Dial.2, Wiper.30wpm	In(Low), In(2)
6	Lever.Low, Dial.2, Wiper.30wpm	e3: move dial up one position	Lever.Low, Dial.3, Wiper.30wpm	In(Low), In(3)
7	Lever.Low, Dial.3, Wiper.30wpm	e2: move lever down one position	Lever.Int, Dial.3, Wiper. Int.20wpm	In(Int), In(3)
8	Lever.Int, Dial.3, Wiper. Int.20wpm	e2: move lever down one position	Lever.Off, Dial.3, Wiper.0wpm	In(Off), In(3)

Table 9.6 Representation of Behavioral Issues with Statecharts

Issue	*Represented?*	*Example*
Sequence	yes	Sequential blobs
Selection	yes	A blob with two emanating transitions
Repetition	yes	A transition going back to a "previous" blob
Enable	yes	The st(A) [Activity A is started] language element
Disable	yes	The sp(A) [Activity A is stopped] language element
Trigger	yes	The st!(A) [Activate the activity A] language element
Activate	yes	The sp!(A) [Terminate the activity A] language element
Suspend	yes	The sd!(A) [Suspend the activity A] language element
Resume	yes	The rs!(A) [Resume the activity A] language element
Pause	yes	(Suspend followed by resume)
Conflict	yes	Determined from an execution table by the choice of which event occurs
Priority	yes	Transition from preferred blob to other blob(s)
Mutual exclusion	yes	Concurrent regions
Concurrent execution	yes	Concurrent regions
Deadlock	...	Determined from an execution table
Context-sensitive input events	yes	As in finite state machines
Multiple-context output events	yes	As in finite state machines
Asynchronous events	yes	Concurrent regions
Event quiescence	yes	Determined from an execution table

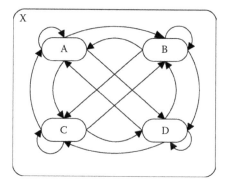

Figure 9.14   A complete graph of four nodes.

transitions. As a result, it is more difficult to perform a technical inspection of a complex statechart. Table 9.6 lists the behavioral issues with statecharts.

References

Harel, D. 1988. On visual formalisms. *Communications of the ACM 31* (5): 514–530.

Exercises

1. Express the Windchill Factor Table problem as a statechart. Discuss how well the problem is represented.
2. Express the Previous Date problem as a statechart. Discuss how well the problem is represented.
3. Express the Saturn Cruise Control problem as a statechart. Discuss how well the problem is represented.
4. Express the Programmable Thermostat problem as a statechart. Discuss how well the problem is represented.
5. Express the Railroad Crossing Gate Controller problem as a statechart. Discuss how well the problem is represented.
6. Express the Six-Coin Espresso Vending Machine (see Chapter 3) as a statechart. Compare your statechart to the one in the text. Does the simplification make the statechart model any more useful?
7. Referring to Figure 9.7 and Table 9.1:
   - Is there a sequence of events that will extend the scenario in Table 9.1 to the initial set of active states B, F, J?
   - Make an execution table for the input event sequence e, f, n. (Be sure to consider output events that later are input events.)
8. Figure 9.14 shows what is known as a Complete Directed Graph, in which every node has an edge to every other node, including itself. Show how you could simplify this using elements of the statechart notation.

Chapter 10

Object-Oriented Models

The Unified Modeling Language (UML) from the Object Management Group (see www.omg.org for more details) is the *de facto* standard for object modeling. In version UML 2.0 there are three categories of models—those that describe structure, behavior, and interaction. One of the main contributions of UML is the blending of the Is (structure) and the Does (behavior) views, as discussed in Chapter 1. For the sake of completeness, the full list of UML 2.0 diagrams is listed here (OMG 2008).

Structural models
- Class diagram
- Object diagram
- Component diagram
- Composite-structure diagram
- Package diagram
- Deployment diagram

Behavioral models
- Use-case diagram
- Activity diagram
- State-machine diagram

Interaction models
- Sequence diagram
- Communication diagram
- Timing diagram
- Interaction-overview diagram

There are distinct schools of thought on using UML for software development. The top-down school begins with structural models (primarily class diagrams) and then moves on to behavioral models (use case diagram, activity diagrams, and state machine diagrams). The bottom-up school starts with behavioral models, and uses them to help identify structural components. Both approaches work, and the choice is really one of personal style and taste.

10.1 Notation and Technique

In this chapter we focus on the requirements level, behavioral models:

- Use case diagram
- Activity diagram
- State machine diagram
- Sequence diagram

The use case diagram simply provides an overview of the connections among actors (sources and destinations of system-level inputs and outputs) with individual use cases. In some ways, this is reminiscent of the Context Diagram of (Yourdon style) Structured Analysis. Activity diagrams are a blend of ordinary Petri nets and flowcharts. As such, they are intuitively obvious, easy to create, and easily understood. The state machine diagram of choice is a simplified version of statecharts (see Chapter 9). Finally, there is the sequence diagram, which is one of the few models anywhere that directly combines the Is and Does views.

10.1.1 Use Case Diagrams

Use cases are an excellent way for customers/users and developers to communicate the Does view of a system. There is a whole taxonomy of use cases, based generally on level of detail (Larman 1998). Here is a sample use case for the Saturn Windshield Wiper.

Use Case Name:	Lever Up
Use Case ID:	L1
Initiating Actor(s):	Lever
Description:	Car driver moves the windshield lever up one position, *e.g.,* from the Off to the Intermittent position.
Preconditions:	1. An initial lever position: one of Off, Int, or Low

Event Sequence:	1.	Car driver moves the windshield lever up one position.
	2.1.	If the Dial position is 1, the system delivers 6 wipes per minute.
	2.2.	If the Dial position is 2, the system delivers 12 wipes per minute.
	2.3.	If the Dial position is 3, the system delivers 20 wipes per minute.
	2.4.	If the lever is at Low, the system delivers 30 wipes per minute.
	2.5.	If the lever is at High, the system delivers 60 wipes per minute.
Receiving Actor(s):	None	
Postconditions:	1. Lever position is one of Int, Low, or High	
Source of Use Case:	Problem statement	

Once a set of use cases has been defined, the use case diagram shows how the individual use cases are related to external actors, which are sources of system-level inputs and destinations of system-level outputs. Figure 10.1 shows a sample use case diagram (with three other, not defined here, use cases) for the Saturn Windshield Wiper.

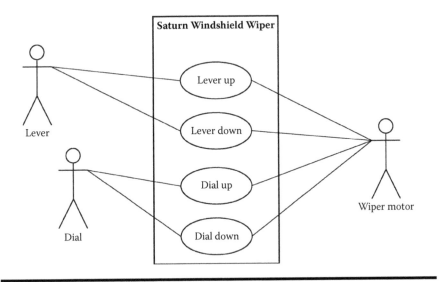

Figure 10.1 Use case diagram for the Saturn Windshield Wiper.

Development based on use case definition is strictly a bottom-up, behavior-based approach. How many use cases are necessary (or even sufficient) is an unavoidable question. The easy answer is when the customer/user is satisfied with an existing set of use cases, but this may or may not meet the needs of developers and system testers. There are better answers, based on some notion of coverage. Consider a set of use cases that covers (choose a level or a combination of levels):

■ All system-level inputs
■ All system-level outputs
■ All classes
■ All messages

UML 2.0 allows connections among use cases in a use case diagram. For example, one use case may use another, or a use case may extend (be a special case of) another. One problem with the use case diagram is that it does not scale up very well.

10.1.2 Activity Diagrams

The UML 2.0 activity diagram provides a closer look at the implementation of a single use case. The most interesting part of an activity diagram is the use of partitions, also called swim lanes, to show the devices or classes that perform activities. Figure 10.2 shows the symbols used in UML 2.0 activity diagrams.

There are two conventions for activity diagrams: horizontal and vertical. In the horizontal version, an activity begins with an initial state in the upper left corner of the diagram, and generally proceeds from left to right, as in (Western) reading style. The vertical style is more common when partitions (swim lanes) are used to designate either classes or agents that support the use case.

The symbol set suggests, correctly so, that activity diagrams are extensions of the basic idea of flowcharts to an object-oriented paradigm. The main difference is the use of the transition symbol, which acts almost like a Petri net transition. The

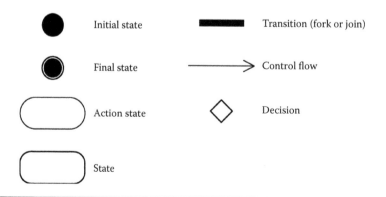

Figure 10.2   Symbols used in activity diagrams.

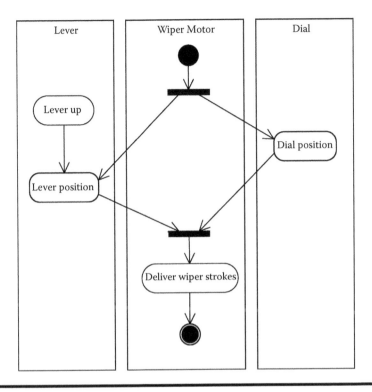

Figure 10.3   Activity diagram for sample use case.

fork and join possibilities refer to transitions having, respectively, several outputs and several inputs. More specifically, a forked transition corresponds exactly to the Petri net synchronized start, and a joined transition corresponds exactly to the Petri net synchronized stop (see Chapter 7). Figure 10.3 shows an activity chart for the Saturn Windshield Wiper use case described earlier.

Because activity diagrams are "object-oriented flowcharts," they inevitably have all the limitations of ordinary flowcharts. They do not express events well (in Figure 10.3, we use an action state to indicate that an event causes a change in lever position). The fact that they only show one sequence is not a limitation, because they are intentionally at the single use case level.

10.1.3 State Machine Diagrams

Statecharts—and their special, simplified case, finite state machines—are the control model central to UML 2.0. A statechart is developed for each class, and therefore summarizes how a class participates in overall system behavior. One fundamental problem: There is no general way to compose statecharts into larger statecharts that represent behavior at the scope of two or more classes.

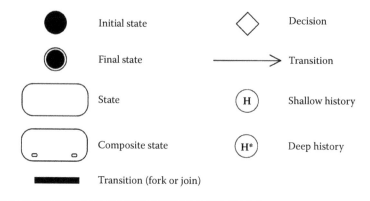

Figure 10.4 Symbols used in UML statecharts.

Several UML statechart symbols (see Figure 10.4) are identical to those used in UML activity charts; this is deliberate. Personally, I do not see much use for the decision symbol in a statechart. The state symbol is used for ordinary states, as in finite state machines. The composite state symbol is used when a state contains lower level states, as in the full statechart notation. Technically, composite states can be used to describe concurrent regions, again as with the original statechart notation. This is seldom used, however, because the UML assumption is that a particular class is being described. The shallow and deep history symbols are really directed toward tool support. A shallow history node contains the previous state of an object, and a deep history node contains the full history of an object.

10.1.4 Sequence Diagrams

The UML sequence diagram is unique in the world of mainline models: It combines both the Is and the Does views of a single use case. In a UML sequence diagram, an object from each class needed to implement the use case has an object lifeline, which refers to the execution time during which the object is instantiated. Lifelines are vertical dashed lines, with the name of the object/class at the top. The remaining symbols refer to the message-based communication among the objects (see Figure 10.5).

In a UML sequence diagram, we picture time as flowing downward. One variation of activity diagrams is to enlarge the dashed line to a narrow rectangle to show when an object is instantiated and when it is destroyed. Since a sequence diagram refers to a single use case, it shows the message-based interaction among objects instantiated at execution time from the classes that support the use case. The objects/classes represent the Is view, and the sequence of messages and message returns captures the execution-time Does view.

The sequence diagram in Figure 10.6 presumes the existence of four supporting classes—Lever, Controller, Dial, and Wiper. In Figure 10.6, the sequence begins

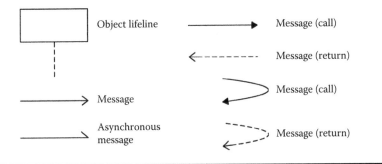

Figure 10.5   UML sequence diagram symbols.

with the lever event described as event 1 in the Event Sequence part of the use case given earlier. A "lever event" is somewhat vague, but that is the way it is expressed in the use case. We could have been very specific and described several lever events:

- e1.1: move lever from Off to Int
- e1.2: move lever from Int to Low
- e1.3: move lever from Low to High
- e2.1: move lever from High to Low
- e2.2: move lever from Low to Int
- e2.3: move lever from Int to Off

This would yield six use cases, and each use case would need to have preconditions referring to the dial position. This issue of use case granularity echoes the discussion (see Chapter 3) of generalized events, which frequently are context sensitive, versus a related list of context-specific events. At the requirements level, the generalized form

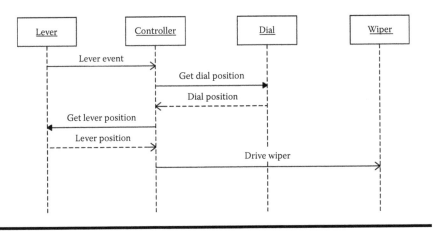

Figure 10.6   Sequence diagram for the sample use case.

reduces the number of use cases, and thereby enhances system comprehension. At the same time, however, a system tester would prefer more specific use cases.

10.2 Examples

Because the UML 2.0 models do not really add much to what we have already discussed more thoroughly in the preceding chapters, we will just comment on which models would be appropriate for the five examples.

10.2.1 Simplified U.S. 1040EZ Income Tax Form

Except for the choice of order (deductions first or income first), the 1040EZ form would be described with one use case. The corresponding activity diagram would be nearly identical to the flowchart in Chapter 4. The statechart for the single use case would have all the unnecessary complexity that we saw in Chapter 9. Finally, we could imagine classes for Deductions, Income sources, and the tax table, resulting in a sequence diagram with three classes. All of this is technical obfuscation—far more complex than necessary.

10.2.2 The NextDate Function

Using UML for the NextDate function will be very similar to the problems just discussed for the 1040EZ problem: technical overkill. We could imagine a Date class that is an aggregation of Day, Month, and Year classes. The latter three classes would take care of range validation, and the Date class would deal with date validity and date incrementing. Except for the order in which the day, month, and year values are processed, NextDate will have one use case. The activity diagram will be very similar to the flowchart in Chapter 4, and the statechart will be as unsatisfactory as the one in Chapter 9. Finally, the single use case will have four classes, so the sequence diagram will simply show a sequence of Get messages from Date to Day, Month, and Year.

10.2.3 Espresso Vending Machine

The Espresso Vending Machine example is a perfect place to have a discussion about short versus long use cases. Go back and look at all the paths in Figure 6.6. Each path would have a full use case, and the UML modeling would be both voluminous and boring. In the early days of computing, Richard Hamming once wrote that "the purpose of computing is insight, not numbers." This extends to modeling: We seek insight, not massive redundancy. A short use case is at the state transition level in Figure 6.6. The precondition is the state proposition of the originating state, and the postcondition is the state proposition of the terminating state. The event sequence is the event that causes the transition, and, if there are any outputs associated with the transition, they are either output events or actions. Short use cases then "connect" at their postcondition/precondition boundaries. The result is a significantly smaller set of very simple use cases, each of which will have correspondingly simple activity diagrams, statecharts, and sequence diagrams.

Here is a "medium length" use case for the Espresso Vending Machine:

Use Case Name:	Two € 0.50 coins
Use Case ID:	Espresso1
Initiating Actor(s):	Coin slot
Description:	Customer inserts two €0.50 coins and receives a cup of espresso.
Preconditions:	1. Coin total is €0.00.
Event Sequence:	1. A €0.50 coin is inserted. 2. A second €0.50 coin is inserted. 3. A cup of espresso is dispensed.
Receiving Actor(s):	Espresso vending machine
Postconditions:	1. Coin total is €0.00. 2. Cup of espresso is waiting for customer.
Source of Use Case:	Problem statement

Assuming we had classes for CoinSlot, EspressoMachine, and Dispenser, the corresponding UML sequence diagram is in Figure 10.7; the more detailed activity diagram is in Figure 10.8. These figures are for one use case. Considering the potentially large number of use cases for an application, the UML sequence diagrams and activity diagrams will be very space consuming and not particularly enlightening. A single statechart will be more helpful, and it will be extremely similar to Figure 9.10. (Why not identical? UML statecharts have a trivially different symbol set.)

In fairness, it might be worthwhile to select short use cases and combine them into the more traditional long use cases that span the set of states in Figure 6.6. Even then, there will be a lot of redundancy in the resulting UML behavioral models.

10.2.4 Smart Fuel Pump

As we saw in Chapter 9, statecharts are an optimal choice for the Smart Fuel Pump problem; see Figure 9.12 for the statechart model of the fuel pump. We can postulate several short use cases; here is a partial list:

UC1: attendant approval   UC2: attendant rejection
UC3: credit card approval   UC4: credit card rejection

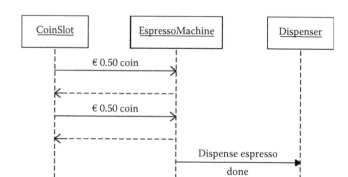

Figure 10.7   Sequence diagram for use case Espresso1.

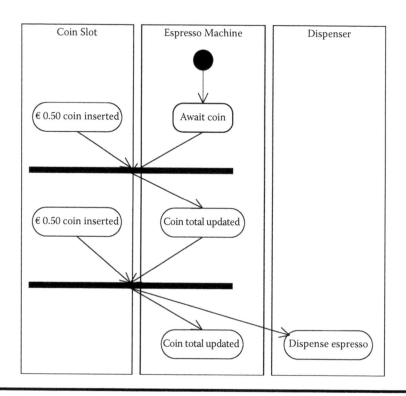

Figure 10.8   Activity diagram for use case Espresso1.

UC5:   fuel grade selection (this could be subdivided into three fuel-type use cases)
UC6:   nozzle removal   UC7:   nozzle replacement
UC8:   trigger squeeze   UC9:   trigger release
UC10: display update   UC11: 4% tank level event
UC12: attendant payment   UC13: credit card payment

In a full UML model, each of these would have an activity diagram, and these diagrams would refer to classes such as these: FuelPump (an aggregate of Display, Nozzle, and Trigger), Attendant, CreditCardCompany, and Tank. Figure 10.9 is a use case diagram for these use cases and actors that correspond to the classes.

One of the problems with UML is that, even for such a small example, 13 activity diagrams represent a lot of effort for little benefit. Similarly, UML sequence diagrams, on a per use case basis, are not very helpful. One conclusion: While

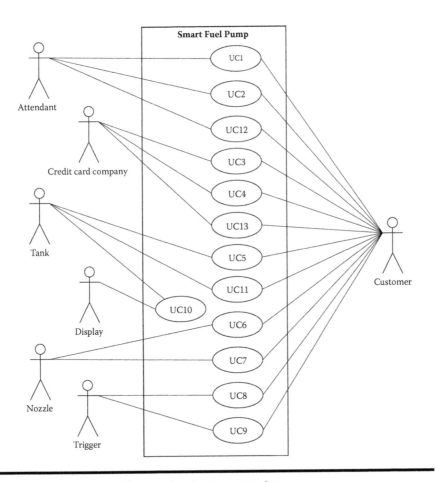

Figure 10.9   Use case diagram for the Smart Fuel Pump.

Table 10.1   Representation of Behavioral Issues with UML

Issue	Represented?	Example
Sequence	yes	Sequential blobs
Selection	yes	A blob with two emanating transitions
Repetition	yes	A transition going back to a "previous" blob
Enable	no	…
Disable	no	…
Trigger	no	…
Activate	no	…
Suspend	no	…
Resume	no	…
Pause	no	…
Conflict	yes	Determined from an execution table by the choice of which event occurs
Priority	yes	Transition from preferred blob to other blob(s)
Mutual exclusion	yes	Concurrent regions
Concurrent execution	yes	Concurrent regions
Deadlock	…	Determined from an execution table
Context-sensitive input events	yes	As in finite state machines
Multiple-context output events	yes	As in finite state machines
Asynchronous events	yes	Concurrent regions
Event quiescence	yes	Determined from an execution table

statecharts clearly scale up very well to large systems, the other behavioral diagrams do not.

10.2.5 *Saturn Windshield Wiper Controller*

The UML diagrams for the Saturn Windshield Wiper Controller are done elsewhere:

- Figure 10.1 is the use case diagram.
- Figure 10.3 is the activity diagram.
- Figure 10.6 is the sequence diagram.
- Figure 9.13 is the statechart.

10.3 Advantages and Limitations

Because UML uses the statechart notation, we would expect that the representation of behavioral issues would be identical to that of statecharts in Chapter 9. This is not quite the case: Several of the ESML (Extended Systems Modeling Language) issues are implemented in the elaborate transition language of the original statecharts; they are not part of UML 2.0. Table 10.1 shows the behavioral issues with UML.

References

Larman, C. 1998. *Applying UML and patterns: An introduction to object-oriented analysis and design.* Upper Saddle River, N.J.: Prentice Hall.
OMG. 2008. Object Management Group. Introduction to OMG's Unified Modeling Language. http://www.omg.org/gettingstarted/what_is_uml.htm.

Exercises

1. Try doing a "full" UML description of the Espresso Vending Machine. What insights do you get from these models?
   - Use case diagram
   - Activity diagram
   - State machine diagram
   - Sequence diagram

Chapter 11

Model Comparisons

"My object all sublime, I shall achieve in time—To let the punishment fit the crime."

—Mikado, in Gilbert and Sullivan's The Mikado

Crime and punishment seem pretty dramatic for applications and models, but the sentiment is correct: The theme of this book has been to find a good match between problems and models. So far we have examined five diverse problems and expressed them with six models (seven, if we count UML). In the process, we noted the advantages and disadvantages of each modeling technique with respect to each of the problems.

The behavioral issues identified in Chapter 3 are recapitulated in Table 11.1 with respect to the possibility of a model representing the issue.

11.1 Selecting an Appropriate Model

Given an application, Table 11.1 provides a simple way to select an appropriate model, where "appropriate" has a sense of necessary and sufficient. We would like all the important aspects of a problem to be represented, and at the same time, we want the model to be as simple as possible.

11.1.1 Simplified U.S. 1040EZ Income Tax Form

As we saw in Chapter 4, the only behavioral issues for the Simplified U.S. 1040EZ Income Tax Form problem are selection and repetition. We also noted that the

Table 11.1 Behavioral Issues Represented in Models

Issues	Flowcharts	Decision Tables	FSMs	Petri Nets	EDPNs	Statecharts
Sequence	yes	no	yes	yes	yes	yes
Selection	yes	yes	yes	yes	yes	yes
Repetition	yes	yes	yes	yes	yes	yes
Enable	no	no	no	yes	yes	yes
Disable	no	no	no	yes	yes	yes
Trigger	no	no	no	yes	yes	yes
Activate	no	no	no	yes	yes	yes
Suspend	no	no	no	yes	yes	yes
Resume	no	no	no	yes	yes	yes
Pause	no	no	no	yes	yes	yes
Conflict	no	no	no	yes	yes	yes
Priority	no	no	no	yes	yes	yes
Mutual exclusion	no	yes	no	yes	yes	yes
Concurrent execution	no	no	no	yes	yes	yes
Deadlock	no	no	no	yes	yes	yes
Context-sensitive input events	no	yes	yes	not nicely	yes	yes
Multiple-context output events	yes	yes	yes	not nicely	yes	yes
Asynchronous events	no	no	no	not nicely	yes	yes
Event quiescence	no	no	no	not nicely	yes	yes

problem involves some computation—not strictly a behavioral issue, but certainly a modeling issue. Table 11.2 is a reduction of Table 11.1 to just the issues of the U.S. 1040EZ problem. Each of the models except decision tables is sufficient, but finite state machines (FSMs), ordinary and event-driven Petri nets (EDPNs), and statecharts are all excessive. The appropriate choice is clear: flowcharts.

Table 11.2   Behavioral Issues in the Simplified U.S. 1040EZ Income Tax Form Problem

Issues	U.S. 1040EZ	Flowcharts	Decision Tables	FSMs	Petri Nets	EDPNs	Statecharts
Sequence	x	yes	no	yes	yes	yes	yes
Selection	x	yes	yes	yes	yes	yes	yes
Repetition	...	yes	yes	yes	yes	yes	yes

11.1.2 The NextDate Function

Recall from Chapter 5 that the only behavioral issues with the NextDate problem are sequence and selection, and the sequential part is minimal (see Table 11.3). The real issue is that the three variables, Month, Day, and Year, are not independent variables. Decision tables highlight the consequences of these dependencies; hence they are the best choice.

Once again, finite state machines, ordinary and event-driven Petri nets, and statecharts are all excessive, and flowcharts do not facilitate the analysis of the dependencies among the three variables.

11.1.3 Espresso Vending Machine

The Espresso Vending Machine is an event-driven system, and it contains highly sequential behaviors. These two properties rule out flowcharts and decision tables. Table 11.4 shows the behavioral issues of the Espresso Vending Machine. Flowcharts

Table 11.3   Behavioral Issues in the NextDate Function

Issues	NextDate	Flowcharts	Decision Tables	FSMs	Petri Nets	EDPNs	Statecharts
Sequence	(x)	yes	no	yes	yes	yes	yes
Selection	x	yes	yes	yes	yes	yes	yes
Repetition	...	yes	yes	yes	yes	yes	yes

Table 11.4 Behavioral Issues in the Espresso Vending Machine

Issues	Espresso Machine	Flowcharts	Decision Tables	FSMs	Petri Nets	EDPNs	Statecharts
Sequence	x	yes	no	yes	yes	yes	yes
Selection	x	yes	yes	yes	yes	yes	yes
Context-sensitive input events	x	no	yes	yes	not nicely	yes	yes
Multiple-context output events	x	yes	yes	yes	not nicely	yes	yes
Event quiescence	x	no	no	no	not nicely	yes	yes

and decision tables both fall short, for different reasons. Finite state machines are better, but they don't show event quiescence. Ordinary Petri nets don't deal explicitly with events, and event-driven markings are not supported, so they are ruled out. That leaves event-driven Petri nets and statecharts as possible choices. If event quiescence is not a concern, finite state machines would be the appropriate choice. Why? For one reason, they are simpler than either event-driven Petri nets or statecharts. Also, finite state machines make it a little easier to deal with proscribed behavior, but this gets messy, as we see in the spaghetti-line FSM in Figure 6.6 (Chapter 6). Even though there are no concurrent regions in the problem, the statechart formulation (see Figures 9.10 and 9.11 in Chapter 9) is both simple and complete, and it certainly resolves the scale-up and spaghetti problems of plain finite state machines.

11.1.4 Smart Fuel Pump

The Smart Fuel Pump problem has the richest set of behavioral issues (see Table 11.5). Looking just at this table, flowcharts, decision tables, finite state machines, and ordinary Petri nets are eliminated, leaving only event-driven Petri nets and statecharts. Each model has its merits: The event-driven Petri net (Chapter 8, Figure 8.10) model shows the flow more clearly, and all the event-driven issues are visually obvious. The statechart formulation (Chapter 9, Figure 9.12) has an elegant simplicity, but the actual sequential flows and event issues are less obvious. One big advantage of the statechart model is that global events, such as the 4%

Table 11.5   Behavioral Issues in the Smart Fuel Pump

Issues	Smart Fuel Pump	Flowcharts	Decision Tables	FSMs	Petri Nets	EDPNs	Statecharts
Sequence	x	yes	no	yes	yes	yes	yes
Selection	x	yes	yes	yes	yes	yes	yes
Repetition	x	yes	yes	yes	yes	yes	yes
Enable	x	no	no	no	yes	yes	yes
Disable	x	no	no	no	yes	yes	yes
Trigger	x	no	no	no	yes	yes	yes
Activate	x	no	no	no	yes	yes	yes
Suspend	x	no	no	no	yes	yes	yes
Resume	x	no	no	no	yes	yes	yes
Pause	x	no	no	no	yes	yes	yes
Context-sensitive input events	x	no	yes	yes	not nicely	yes	yes
Asynchronous events	x	no	no	no	not nicely	yes	yes
Event quiescence	x	no	no	no	not nicely	yes	yes

tank level event, are shown with just one edge (transition) rather than the numerous inputs needed in a full event-driven Petri net. This one is almost a toss-up.

11.1.5 Saturn Windshield Wiper Controller

The Saturn Windshield Wiper Controller problem is also an event-driven system, so we would expect it to be very similar to the Smart Fuel Pump problem. Table 11.6 shows the behavioral issues in the Saturn Windshield Wiper Controller problem. One difference is that the lever and dial devices can execute concurrently, which clearly favors the statechart choice. Flowcharts, decision tables, finite state machines, and ordinary Petri nets all fall short, and we would have to make some sort of assignment of EDPN events, places, and transitions to parallel devices.

Table 11.6 Behavioral Issues in the Saturn Windshield Wiper Controller Problem

Issues	Windshield Wiper	Flowcharts	Decision Tables	FSMs	Petri Nets	EDPNs	Statecharts
Sequence	x	yes	no	yes	yes	yes	yes
Selection	x	yes	yes	yes	yes	yes	yes
Repetition	x	yes	yes	yes	yes	yes	yes
Enable	x	no	no	no	yes	yes	yes
Disable	x	no	no	no	yes	yes	yes
activate	x	no	no	no	yes	yes	yes
Context-sensitive input events	x	no	yes	yes	not nicely	yes	yes
Asynchronous events	x	no	no	no	not nicely	yes	yes
Event quiescence	x	no	no	no	not nicely	yes	yes

11.2 A Formal Consolidation of Executable Models

In this section, we shall see that the executable models (decision tables, finite state machines, ordinary and event-driven Petri nets, and statecharts) can all be reduced to propositional syllogisms. Even more surprising, model execution maps into syllogistic inference.

11.2.1 Modus Ponens

Modus ponens is a fundamental rule of inference in formal logic. It is the syllogism:

$$p \rightarrow q \quad \text{(If p, Then q)}$$
$$\underline{p} \quad\quad \underline{p}$$
$$\therefore q \quad\quad \text{Therefore q}$$

There is a closely related syllogism that deals with the transitivity of the If, Then connective:

$$p \rightarrow q$$
$$\underline{q \rightarrow r}$$
$$\therefore p \rightarrow r$$

We can check whether or not a syllogism is valid by restating it in the form of If (premises) Then (conclusion). If that result is a tautology, then the syllogism is valid (and conversely!). Here is a check for the validity of *modus ponens*:

p	q	$p \rightarrow q$	$(p \rightarrow q) \wedge p$	$((p \rightarrow q) \wedge p) \rightarrow q$
T	T	T	T	T
T	F	F	F	T
F	T	T	F	T
F	F	T	F	T

We will use Railroad Crossing Gate Controller (see Chapter 3) as a continuing example. Since ordinary Petri nets are a special case of event-driven Petri nets, they will not be cast into syllogisms here. The input events, output events, and states are:

p1: train arrival   p2: train departure
p3: lower gate   p4: raise gate

s1: 0 trains in crossing   s2: 1 train in crossing
s3: 2 trains in crossing   s4: 3 trains in crossing

We will execute the scenario <p1, p1, p2, p1, p2, p2> with the precondition s1: 0 trains in crossing and postcondition s1: 0 trains in crossing.

11.2.2 Casting a Decision Table into a Propositional Syllogism

Given a decision table, follow this procedure to construct its corresponding propositional syllogism:

1. Each rule R is mapped to a distinct proposition that describes the conditions C(R) and a set of actions A(R) to be performed. A decision table has propositions of the form C(R) → A(R)
2. Each rule becomes a (compound) proposition C(R) in which conditions become clauses:
   - If condition c_i is true, the proposition uses c_i.
   - If condition c_i is false, the proposition uses ~c_i.
   - If condition c_i is a Don't Care condition, the proposition omits c_i.
   - C(R) is the conjunction of these clauses.
3. Form rule action sets A(R) as follows:
   - If action a_i is performed, then $a_i \in$ A(R).
   - A(R) is the conjunction of the actions.

Railroad Crossing Gate Controller Decision Table

Condition	R1	R2	R3	R4	R5	R6	R7	R8
c1: 0 trains	T	T	F!	F!	F!	F!	F!	F!
c2: 1 train	F!	F!	T	T	F!	F!	F!	F!
c3: 2 trains	F!	F!	F!	F!	T	T	F!	F!
c4: 3 trains	F!	F!	F!	F!	F!	F!	T	T
c4: arrival	T	F!	T	F!	T	F!	T	F!
c6: departure	F!	T	F!	T	F!	T	F!	T
a1: lower gate	x	—	—	—	—	—	—	—
a2: raise gate	—	—	—	x	—	—	—	—
a3: do nothing	—	—	x	—	x	x	—	x
a4: impossible	—	x	—	—	—	—	x	—

The full decision table reduces to the following eight propositions (one for each rule):

C(R1) → A(R1) is (0 trains ∧ arrival) → (lower gate ∧ 1 train)

C(R2) → A(R2) is (0 trains ∧ departure) → (impossible)

C(R3) → A(R3) is (1 train ∧ arrival) → (2 trains)

C(R4) → A(R4) is (1 train ∧ departure) → (raise gate ∧ 0 trains)

C(R5) → A(R5) is (2 trains ∧ arrival) → (do nothing ∧ 3 trains)

C(R6) → A(R6) is (2 trains ∧ departure) → (do nothing ∧ 1 train)

C(R7) → A(R7) is (3 trains ∧ arrival) → (impossible)

C(R8) → A(R8) is (3 trains ∧ departure) → (do nothing ∧ 2 trains)

Rules are selected by the occurrence of events and postconditions of the previous rule execution, so we have short syllogisms for each rule. (If an impossible rule is selected, i.e., R2 or R7, no action occurs.)

Rule 1 execution:

arrival	(event occurs)
0 trains	(initial condition)
∴(0 trains ∧ arrival)	(conjunction)
(0 trains ∧ arrival) → (lower gate ∧ 1 train)	(*modus ponens*)
∴(lower gate ∧ 1 train)	

Rule 3 execution:

arrival	(event occurs)
1 train	(initial condition)
∴.(1 train ∧ arrival)	(conjunction)
(1 train ∧ arrival) → (do nothing ∧ 2 trains)	(*modus ponens*)
∴ (do nothing ∧ 2 trains)	

Rule 4 execution:

departure	(event occurs)
1 train	(initial condition)
∴.(1 train ∧ departure)	(conjunction)
(1 train ∧ departure) → (raise gate ∧ 0 trains)	(*modus ponens*)
∴ (raise gate ∧ 0 trains)	

The syllogisms for Rules R6 and R8 are similar to that for Rule R4, except the numbers of trains are changed. The syllogism for Rule R5 is similar to that for Rule R3.

11.2.3 Casting a Finite State Machine into a Propositional Syllogism

Given a finite state machine (S, T, E, A), follow this procedure to construct its corresponding propositional syllogism:

1. Determine the state proposition P(s) for each s in the state set S.
2. Determine the transition proposition P(t) for each t in the state transition set T.
3. Indicate an initial state by noting that the corresponding state proposition is true.

Figure 11.1 is a slight revision of Figure 6.1, showing the finite state machine for the railroad crossing gate controller:

The state propositions are obvious:

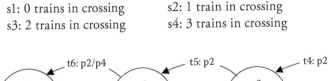

s1: 0 trains in crossing   s2: 1 train in crossing
s3: 2 trains in crossing   s4: 3 trains in crossing

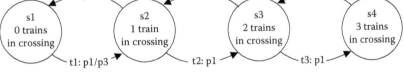

Figure 11.1   Finite state machine for the Railroad Crossing Gate Controller.

This FSM only shows prescribed behavior (p2 cannot occur in state s1, and p1 cannot occur in state s4), so there are only six transition propositions. Execution of a finite state machine is more elegant than decision table execution, and this extends to the corresponding syllogistic inferences. We take that the transition propositions are numbered premises, and then number the premises that correspond to the event sequence. Rather than show the conjunction inferences, we just show the conjunction of a state proposition with a corresponding event from the event sequence <p1, p1, p1, p2, p2, p2>. It seems odd to have premises repeated (like 8, 9, 11 and 10, 12, 13). Since these refer to discrete events, we can "use" an event premise when it is no longer available.

(1) $P(t1) = (s1) \wedge p1 \rightarrow ((s2) \wedge$ lower gate)
(2) $P(t2) = (s2) \wedge p1 \rightarrow (s3)$
(3) $P(t3) = (s3) \wedge p1 \rightarrow (s4)$
(4) $P(t4) = (s4) \wedge p2 \rightarrow (s3)$
(5) $P(t5) = (s3) \wedge p2 \rightarrow (s2)$
(6) $P(t6) = (s2) \wedge p2 \rightarrow ((s1) \wedge$ raise gate)
(7) s1   (initial condition)
(8) p1
(9) p1
(10) p1
(11) p2
(12) p2
(13) p2

Executing the finite state machine maps into the following (long) syllogistic deduction:

(1) $(s1) \wedge p1 \rightarrow ((s2) \wedge$ lower gate)
(7) s1   (initial condition)
(8) p1 _____
(14) $\therefore ((s2) \wedge$ lower gate)
(15) $\therefore (s2)$ (immediate inference)
(2) $(s2) \wedge p1 \rightarrow (s3)$
(9) p1 _____
(16) $\therefore (s3)$
(3) $(s3) \wedge p1 \rightarrow (s4)$
(10) p1 _____
(17) $\therefore (s4)$
(4) $(s4) \wedge p2 \rightarrow (s3)$
(11) p2 _____

(18) ∴ (s3)
(5) (s3) ∧ p2 → (s2)
(12) p2_____
(19) ∴ (s2)
(6) (s2) ∧ p2 → ((s1) ∧ raise gate)
(13) p2_____
(20) ∴ ((s1) ∧ raise gate)

11.2.4 Casting an Event-Driven Petri Net into a Propositional Syllogism

Since ordinary Petri nets are a special case of event-driven Petri nets, we only consider the latter here. Given an event-driven Petri net (P, D, T, In, Out), follow this procedure to construct its corresponding propositional syllogism:

1. Each transition t_i in an EDPN with input event p_i and data place d_i, and output event p_k and data place d_k, is mapped into the proposition:

$$t_i : p_i \land d_i \rightarrow p_k \land d_k$$

2. If there are more than one input events, data places, or output events, take the conjunction of these. For example, transition t_x has three input events, two input places, two output events, and three output places.

$$t_x : (p_i \land p_j \land p_k) \land (d_p \land d_q) \rightarrow (p_m \land p_n) \land (d_r \land d_s \land d_t)$$

3. If a transition has an inhibitor arc, the negation of the data place proposition is used.

In Figure 11.2, the port input events, port output events, states (as data places), and transitions are all named identically with the corresponding elements in Figure 11.1. Therefore the transition propositions, the premises, and the syllogism are identical to that of the finite state machine for the Railroad Crossing Gate Controller.

11.2.5 Casting a Statechart into a Propositional Syllogism

Since statecharts are an extension of finite state machines, much of the formalism is the same. Transitions in a statechart are always of the form:

$$P(presentState) \land Event(s) \rightarrow P(nextState) \land Action(s)$$

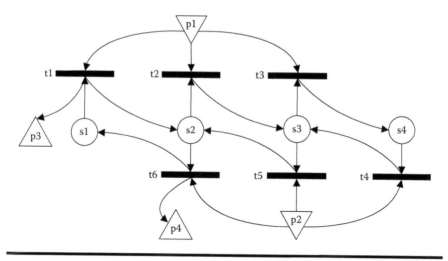

Figure 11.2 Event-driven Petri net for the Railroad Crossing Gate Controller.

Given a statechart, follow this procedure to construct its corresponding propositional syllogism:

1. If a transition is from a simple state to a simple state, the corresponding proposition is

    $$P(presentState) \wedge Event(s) \rightarrow P(nextState) \wedge Action(s)$$

2. If a transition is caused by a language element (see Chapter 9), then that language element is added to the conjunction of states and events that cause the transition.
3. If a transition is from a simple state to a compound state (i.e., one with concurrent regions), P(nextState) is the conjunction of the initial states in each concurrent region.
4. If a transition is from a compound state to a simple state, P(presentState) is the disjunction of the initial states in each concurrent machine.

The statechart for the Railroad Crossing Gate Controller (see Figure 11.3) has no concurrent regions, so the corresponding syllogism will be very similar to that for the ordinary finite state machine.

The transition propositions:

(0) $P(t0) = True \rightarrow s1$
(1) $P(t1) = (p1 \wedge s1) \rightarrow ((Crossing\ occupied \wedge s2) \wedge p3)$
(2) $P(t2) = (p1 \wedge s2) \rightarrow ((Crossing\ occupied \wedge s3)$
(3) $P(t3) = (p1 \wedge s3) \rightarrow ((Crossing\ occupied \wedge s4)$

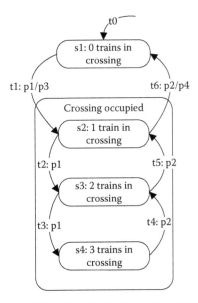

Figure 11.3   Statechart for the Railroad Crossing Gate Controller.

(4) $P(t4) = (p2 \wedge s4) \rightarrow ((\text{Crossing occupied} \wedge s3)$
(5) $P(t5) = (p2 \wedge s3) \rightarrow ((\text{Crossing occupied} \wedge s2)$
(6) $P(t6) = (p2 \wedge s2) \rightarrow (s1 \wedge p4)$
(7)   True (default entry to s1))
(8)   p1
(9)   p1
(10) p1
(11) p2
(12) p2
(13) p2

Except for names, propositions (0) through (13) are identical (as we would expect!) to those in Section 11.2.3 for the finite state machine model. Clearly, the syllogism corresponding to the continuing scenario will also be identical (except for names).

11.2.6 *Benefits of the Formalism*

At first look, the discussion of Section 11.2 seems like technical obfuscation—why bother? There is a mild intellectual satisfaction in knowing that something as dynamic as an executable model can be reduced to something as static as a propositional syllogism. More importantly, this formalism illustrates a mechanism for proving that two models are fundamentally equivalent. Furthermore, if we can prove two models are equivalent, this allows the choice of one over the other for different reasons, perhaps tool availability, or model familiarity. Finally, the formalism might show that something not represented in one model actually is represented in the other.

11.3 Acknowledgment

Early versions of Chapters 1 through 9 were used as a text for the Fall 2008 offering of a graduate course, CS 612 Requirements Specification, at Grand Valley State University, Allendale, Michigan. Throughout the semester, members of the class provided continuing feedback on the chapters as I wrote and distributed them. (I stayed about two weeks ahead of the class!) Here, I thank the class members for their help:

Rick DeVries
Marcia Isserstedt
Michael Lingg
Sindhu Malla
Nikita Parikh
Bert VandenBerg
Craig Witter

Part of the final exam was based on the Pizza Robot problem (from Chapter 3). In one of the questions, students were asked to decide which of the models was most appropriate for the problem. Here is the response from Michael Lingg:

Before discussing which modeling techniques I feel are appropriate for the phone ordering system or the GUI, I want to discuss what I feel each technique is appropriate for.

For flowcharts and decision tables, the question I ask is: Are there states that persist until an external event causes the state to exit and will be reentered at a later time? If so, then a state modeling technique would likely be better than flowcharts or decision tables.

Between flowcharts and decision tables the questions are:

1. Is the sequence of the code important, or do we just want to know what the set of outputs for a set of inputs is?
2. Is the possible number of inputs vs. outputs overly large?

If the sequence is important, then flowcharts are a better modeling technique than decision tables, as decision tables cannot model sequence. Also, if there are a large number of inputs and outputs and little direct mapping, then I feel that flowcharts, even though they will still produce a large flowchart in this situation, produce a cleaner model, as the flowchart can be followed from one place to another, whereas the decision table may require looking at multiple columns and rows to determine the solution.

If sequence is not important and the model created by a decision table can be easily read, then I would model the application with a decision table.

For the state modeling techniques:

I don't see a lot of use for FSMs, as statecharts can do anything an FSM can do (as far as I've seen) and can do it more cleanly as the model grows. In the cases where an FSM would work well, a flowchart seems to be nearly as powerful.

I'm not sure I see Petri nets as a modeling technique for designing code but more of a technique for debugging code execution (before or after implementation). This is because statecharts can do just about anything Petri nets (both event driven and normal) can do and are generally more readable. Petri nets, on the other hand, appear to handle execution, especially with multiple processes, better thanks to the less flexible modeling scheme and each transition having its dependencies directly linked to it. Because I am creating a design model for this project, I will not be using Petri nets.

Having basically knocked out all other models leaves statecharts as the chosen model for any application that works with event-driven states. I feel this model works as one of the best, primarily thanks to its use of sub-states and history.

Telephone ordering system: flowchart

With the above discussion in mind, I feel that the flowchart best models the phone ordering system. This application is very sequential (so the decision table doesn't work very well), the events aren't really asynchronous, and events don't lead to repeating activities except in one location, which doesn't mean a lot because the event isn't really asynchronous, so a statechart would be overkill.

Petri nets could model how this system works fairly effectively, but an execution model isn't likely to be useful given how sequential the application appears to be.

FSMs may work just as well as a flowchart, but I like the flowchart's separate decision and action boxes for this application.

Mike's exam echoes the advice of my father that I mentioned in the Preface: "Use the right tool, and let the tool do the work." Mike learned to make good choices about models, and I hope this book serves you equally effectively.

Exercises

1. Analyze the Wind Chill Factor Table problem in terms of the behavioral issues list in Table 11.1. Which model seems most appropriate?
2. Analyze the Previous Date problem in terms of the behavioral issues list in Table 11.1. Which model seems most appropriate?
3. Analyze the Saturn Cruise Control problem in terms of the behavioral issues list in Table 11.1. Which model seems most appropriate?
4. Analyze the Programmable Thermostat problem in terms of the behavioral issues list in Table 11.1. Which model seems most appropriate?
5. Analyze the Railroad Crossing Gate Controller in terms of the behavioral issues list in Table 11.1. Which model seems most appropriate?

Index

Milton Keynes UK
Ingram Content Group UK Ltd.
UKHW031131141024
449569UK00006B/262